THE SCARS OF DEATH

Children Abducted by the Lord's Resistance Army in Uganda

Human Rights Watch / Africa
Human Rights Watch Children's Rights Project

Human Rights Watch
New York · Washington · London · Brussels

ISBN 1-56432-221-1
Library of Congress Catalog Card Number 97-74724

Human Rights Watch is dedicated to
protecting the human rights of people around the world.

We stand with victims and activists to prevent
discrimination, to uphold political freedom, to protect people from
inhumane conduct in wartime, and to bring offenders to justice.

We investigate and expose
human rights violations and hold abusers accountable.

We challenge governments and those who hold power to end
abusive practices and respect international human rights law.

We enlist the public and the international
community to support the cause of human rights for all.

HUMAN RIGHTS WATCH

ACKNOWLEDGMENTS

This report is based on research in Uganda from late May to early June of 1997. The research was conducted by Rosa Ehrenreich, a consultant for the Human Rights Watch Children's Rights Project, and by Yodon Thonden, counsel for the Children's Rights Project. The report was written by Rosa Ehrenreich, and edited by Yodon Thonden and Lois Whitman, the director of the Children's Rights Project. Peter Takirambudde, the director of Human Rights Watch's Africa Division, and Joanne Mariner, associate counsel for Human Rights Watch, provided additional comments on the manuscript. Linda Shipley, associate to the Children's Rights Project, provided invaluable production assistance.

This report would not have been possible without the assistance of the UNICEF office in Uganda. In particular, we wish to thank Kathleen Cravero, Ponsiano Ochero, Leila Pakkala, and Keith Wright in Kampala, and George Ogol and Moses Ongaria in Gulu. We are also grateful to Professor Semakula Kiwanuka, the Ugandan permanent representative to the United Nations, and to the many Ugandan government officials who facilitated our mission, including Lieutenant Bantariza Shaban, the public relations liasion officer for the Fourth Division of the Uganda People's Defense Force (UPDF), Colonel James Kazini, Commander of the UPDF Fourth Division, and J.J. Odur, the vice-chairman of Gulu's Local Council Five and the chairman of the Gulu Disaster Management Committee.

In Kampala, a number of individuals provided us with helpful background information. They include Richard Young of Red Barnet, Robby Muhumuza of World Vision, Sister Bruna Barolla of the Camboni Sisters, Livingstone Sewanyana of the Foundation for Human Rights Initiative, Cathy Watson, Jim Mugungu of the *Monitor* newspaper, Dr. Fillipo Ciantia of AVSI, the Italian Development Corporation, John Mugisha of the Uganda Law Society, Robina Namusisi of the National Association of Women Lawyers, Regina Lule Mutyaba of the Human Rights Education and Documentation Center, Anna Borzello, the members of the Uganda Human Rights Commission, Hilary Wright, Sister Judith Achilo, Andres Banya of the Acholi Development Association, Hon. Norbert Mao, M.P. for Gulu, Saeed Bukunya of the Office of Child Care and Protection, Hon. Livingstone Okello-Okello, M.P. for Kitgum, Hon. Daniel Omara Atubo, M.P. for Lira, Hon. Alphonse Owiny Dollo, minister of state for the north, Diane Swayles of Save the Children Fund U.K., and Ron and Pam Ferguson of the Mennonite Central Committee.

Outside of Kampala, we were assisted by more people than we can mention here, but especially by Charles Wotmon of World Vision, Paulinus Nyeko of Gulu Human Rights Focus, Sister Rachele Fassera of the St. Mary School in Aboke, Dr. Bruno Correda and Dr. Matthew Lukwiya of Lacor Hospital in Gulu, and the many parents in the Concerned Parents of Aboke organization. We are also grateful to the counselors, teachers and staff at Gulu Save the Children

Organization, World Vision in Gulu and Kiryandongo, and the St. Mary School in Aboke.

Finally, we wish to thank the many Ugandan children who told us their stories. We would thank them each by name, but to do so might endanger their safety. Their courage is an inspiration to us.

CONTENTS

I. SUMMARY AND RECOMMENDATIONS 1

II. THE ABDUCTION OF CHILDREN BY
      THE LORD'S RESISTANCE ARMY 9
    Background 9
    The Children's Stories 12
          Capture and Early Days 13
          On the March in Uganda and Sudan 19
          Life in the Rebel Camps in Sudan 24
          Religion and Ideology 30
          Going into Battle 36
          Escape 39
          The Future 43
    Relevant International Humanitarian Standards 50

III. OTHER EFFECTS OF THE CONFLICT IN THE NORTH 53

IV. THE HISTORY AND CAUSES OF THE CONFLICT 60

V. CONCLUSION 81

APPENDIX A
    Letters from the Aboke School Girls 86

APPENDIX B
    U.N. Convention on the Rights of the Child 97

APPENDIX C
    African Charter on the Rights and Welfare of the Child 118

APPENDIX D
    Draft Optional Protocol to the Convention on
    the Rights of the Child on Involvement of Children
    in Armed Conflicts 133

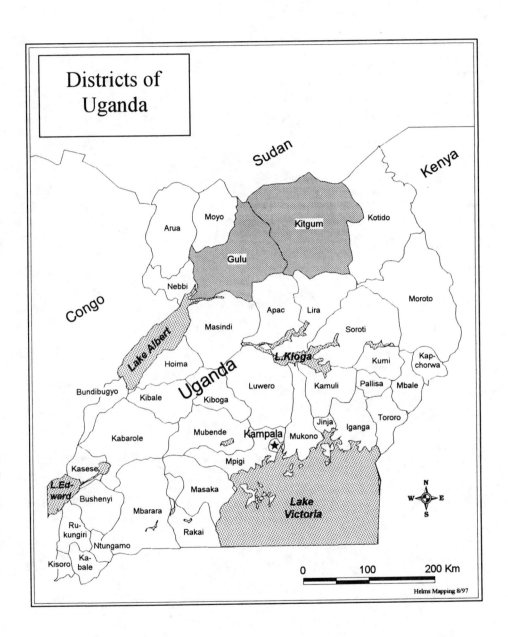

Districts of
Uganda

Sudan

Kenya

Congo

Arua

Moyo

Kitgum

Kotido

Gulu

Nebbi

Moroto

Lake Albert

Apac

Lira

Masindi

Soroti

Hoima

L. Kioga

Uganda

Kumi

Kap-
chorwa

Bundibugyo

Kibale

Luwero

Kamuli

Pallisa

Mbale

Kiboga

Kabarole

Mubende

Tororo

Kampala

Jinja

Iganga

Mukono

Mpigi

Kasese

Masaka

L. Ed-
ward

Bushenyi

Lake
Victoria

Mbarara

Ru-
kungiri

Rakai

Ntungamo

Kisoro

Ka-
bale

N

W   E

S

0   100   200 Km

Helms Mapping 8/97

GLOSSARY

Arabs: a term often used by the children to describe Muslim Sudanese, and/or Sudanese government soldiers.

Dinkas: a people living mostly in Southern Sudan.

Gunship: helicopter.

HSM: Holy Spirit Movement.

Jerrycan: a plastic container used for carrying water and food.

Jok **(plural:** *jogi*): spirit; a powerful supernatural force.

Lakwena: messenger.

LC/RC: local council/resistance committee: terms often used interchangeably to refer to local government committees.

LRA: Lord's Resistance Army. More usually referred to by Ugandans as "the Kony Rebels," or simply "the rebels. "

Malaika: angel.

NGO: nongovernmental organization.

NRA: National Resistance Army. The old name for Yoweri Museveni's soldiers. Although the name has been changed to Uganda People's Defense Force (UPDF), some Ugandans still refer to government soldiers as the National Resistance Army.

Panga: a broad-bladed machete.

RPG: a rocket-propelled grenade.

Simsim: a kind of grain.

SPLA: Sudanese People's Liberation Army.

Tipu: spirit, soul, ghost.

Tipu Maleng: God; the Holy Spirit (usually associated with the Catholic Holy Ghost).

UNICEF: United Nations Children's Fund.

UPDA: Uganda People's Defense Army. A rebel alliance, now defunct. Not to be confused with the similarly named Uganda People's Defense Force (UPDF), the army of the Ugandan government.

UPDF: Uganda People's Defense Force, the army of the Ugandan republic.

I. SUMMARY AND RECOMMENDATIONS

One boy tried to escape, but he was caught. They made him eat a mouthful of red pepper, and five people were beating him. His hands were tied, and then they made us, the other new captives, kill him with a stick. I felt sick. I knew this boy from before. We were from the same village. I refused to kill him and they told me they would shoot me. They pointed a gun at me, so I had to do it. The boy was asking me, "Why are you doing this?" I said I had no choice. After we killed him, they made us smear his blood on our arms. I felt dizzy. There was another dead body nearby, and I could smell the body. I felt so sick. They said we had to do this so we would not fear death and so we would not try to escape.

I feel so bad about the things that I did . . . . It disturbs me so much—that I inflicted death on other people . . . . When I go home I must do some traditional rites because I have killed. I must perform these rites and cleanse myself. I still dream about the boy from my village who I killed. I see him in my dreams, and he is talking to me and saying I killed him for nothing, and I am crying.

- Susan, sixteen

I was good at shooting. I went for several battles in Sudan. The soldiers on the other side would be squatting, but we would stand in a straight line. The commanders were behind us. They would tell us to run straight into gunfire. The commanders would stay behind and would beat those of us who would not run forward. You would just run forward shooting your gun. I don't know if I actually killed any people, because you really can't tell if you're shooting people or not. I might have killed people in the course of the fighting . . . . I remember the first time I was in the front line. The other side started firing, and the commander ordered us to run towards the bullets. I panicked. I saw others falling down dead around me. The commanders were beating us

1

*for not running, for trying to crouch down. They said if we fall
down, we would be shot and killed by the soldiers.*

*In Sudan we were fighting the Dinkas, and other Sudanese
civilians. I don't know why we were fighting them. We were just
ordered to fight.*

- Timothy, fourteen

The Acholi people of northern Uganda have a proverb: "*Poyo too pe
rweny.* " "Death is a scar that never heals. "

In northern Uganda, thousands of children are victims of a vicious cycle
of violence, caught between a brutal rebel group and the army of the Ugandan
government. The rebel Lord's Resistance Army (LRA) is ostensibly dedicated to
overthrowing the government of Uganda, but in practice the rebels appear to
devote most of their time to attacks on the civilian population: they raid villages,
loot stores and homes, burn houses and schools, and rape, mutilate and slaughter
civilians unlucky enough to be in their path.

When the rebels move on, they leave behind the bodies of the dead. But
after each raid, the rebels take away some of those who remain living. In
particular, they take young children, often dragging them away from the dead
bodies of their parents and siblings.

The rebels prefer children of fourteen to sixteen, but at times they abduct
children as young as eight or nine, boys and girls alike. They tie the children to
one another, and force them to carry heavy loads of looted goods as they march
them off into the bush. Children who protest or resist are killed. Children who
cannot keep up or become tired or ill are killed. Children who attempt to escape
are killed.

Their deaths are not quick—a child killed by a single rebel bullet is a
rarity. If one child attempts to escape, the rebels force the other abducted children
to kill the would-be escapee, usually with clubs or machetes. Any child who
refuses to participate in the killing may also be beaten or killed.

The rebels generally bring their captives across the border to a Lord's
Resistance Army camp in Sudan. In the bush in Sudan, a shortage of food and
water reduces many children to eating leaves for survival; deaths from dysentery,
hunger and thirst are frequent. Living conditions in the Lord's Resistance Army
camp are slightly better, because the Sudanese government supplies the Lord's
Resistance Army with both food and arms in exchange for assistance in fighting the
rebel Sudanese People's Liberation Army (SPLA).

Those children who reach the Lord's Resistance Army camp are forced to serve the rebels. Smaller children may be made to run errands, fetch water or cultivate the land; girls as young as twelve are given to rebel commanders as "wives." All of the children are trained as soldiers, taught to use guns and to march.

The Lord's Resistance Army enforces discipline through a combination of violence and threats. Children who do not perform their assigned tasks to the rebels' satisfaction are beaten. Children who flout rebel orders are beaten or killed, often by other abducted children. Failed escape attempts continue to be punished by death, and successful escape attempts lead to retaliation: if one sibling escapes, the rebels often kill the other sibling, or return to the child's home village and slaughter any surviving relatives.

In effect, children abducted by the Lord's Resistance Army become slaves: their labor, their bodies and their lives are all at the disposal of their rebel captors.

Once they have been trained (and sometimes before being trained), the children are forced to fight, both in Uganda and in Sudan. In Sudan, the children are forced to help raid villages for food, and fight against the Sudan People's Liberation Army. In Uganda, the children are also made to loot villages, fight against Ugandan government soldiers, and help abduct other children. When the rebels fight against the Ugandan government army, they force the captive children to the front; children who hang back or refuse to fire are beaten or killed by the rebels, while those who run forward may be mown down by government bullets.

The Lord's Resistance Army's use of children as combatants is an extreme example of a troubling worldwide trend toward increased reliance on child soldiers in conflicts of all sorts. Graca Machel, who headed the United Nations Study on the Impact of Armed Conflict on Children, has pointed out that the proliferation of inexpensive light weapons has contributed to the increased use of children as soldiers:

> [T]he reality is that children have increasingly become targets, and not incidental victims [of war], as a result of conscious and deliberate decisions made by adults. . . . War violates every right of the child. . . . The injury to children—the phsyical wounds, the psychosocial distress, the sexual violence—are affronts to each and every humanitarian impulse that inspired the Convention on the Rights of the Child.

The continued use of child soldiers, says Machel, "demonstrates the failure of the international community to protect and cherish its children."

It is hard to know how many children have been abducted by the rebels. Most estimates suggest that three to five thousand children have escaped from captivity during the past two years. UNICEF estimates that an equal number of children remain in captivity, and an unknown number are dead.

The actions of the Lord's Resistance Army violate the most elementary principles of international humanitarian law. In particular, the rebels stand in blatant violation of Common Article 3 of the Geneva Conventions of 1949, which establishes the minimum rules binding on all parties in internal armed conflicts. Common Article 3 states that people taking no active part in an internal armed conflict (including combatants who are wounded, or who have surrendered or been captured) must be treated humanely, and in particular, it forbids the taking of hostages, the use of murder, mutilation, cruel treatment, torture, and humiliating and degrading treatment.

Escape is rarely the end of an abducted child's ordeal, for those children who escape often find that they have nowhere to go. Their villages may have been destroyed by the rebels; their parents may have been killed or may have fled the countryside for the comparative safety of the towns. Even those children with homes to return to may hesitate to do so, fearing rebel reprisals against them or their families, and ostracism by community members who blame the children for complicity in rebel atrocities. There are few safe havens for these children: two nongovernmental organizations (NGOs) provide live-in trauma counseling centers for escaped abductees, but the centers cannot possibly take in all of the children.

Even those children not captured by rebels suffer the effects of the conflict. The frequent rebel attacks have destabilized the countryside in northern Uganda, destroying the region's agricultural base and wreaking havoc on education and healthcare. Hundreds of village schools have been burned, and scores of health clinics have been raided by rebels desperate to get their hands on medicines. As a result, northern Uganda today faces an acute humanitarian crisis. The two northern districts of Gulu and Kitgum, the homeland of the Acholi people, have been hardest hit; the violence and instability have displaced more than 200,000 northern Ugandans from their rural homes.

The Ugandan government has established a number of "protected camps" near Ugandan army installations, in order to decrease the vulnerability of civilians living in isolated rural areas. Tens of thousands of displaced people have fled the countryside and set up temporary homes in the camps, but crowded conditions and lack of food and sanitation facilities have rendered the population vulnerable to death from malnutrition and disease. Thousands die every month, and despite the nearby military presence, the camps remain targets for rebel attacks.

There is no end in sight. The Lord's Resistance Army's rebellion is deeply rooted in Uganda's troubled history of ethnic conflict, and the war has now dragged on for more than ten years. The last two years have seen a great increase in the scale of the fighting, as a result of Sudanese government support for the Lord's Resistance Army. The Ugandan government army has been unable to combat the rebels effectively, and the prospects for a negotiated peace are bleak.

Children who have escaped from the rebels wake screaming in the night from dreams of pain and death: their dreams are of deaths feared, deaths witnessed, and, all too often, deaths participated in. Perhaps some day, if peace comes, the scars of death will begin to fade. But they will never fully heal.

Recommendations

To the Lord's Resistance Army
- immediately stop abducting children;

- immediately stop killing children;

- immediately stop torturing children;

- immediately stop sexually abusing children;

- immediately release all children remaining in captivity;

- ensure that Lord's Resistance Army combatants respect the human rights of civilians in the areas of conflict.

To the Government of Sudan
- cease all military aid and other support to the Lord's Resistance Army, until it complies with the recommendations outlined above;

- use Sudanese influence over the Lord's Resistance Army to stop the LRA's abduction, killing, torture and sexual abuse of children, to ensure that all LRA captives are treated humanely, and to bring about the immediate release of children held by the LRA;

To the Government of Uganda

•   take all possible steps to protect children from abduction;

•   when fighting the Lord's Resistance Army, take all possible steps to minimize child casualties;

•   ensure that all children who escape or are captured from the rebels receive prompt and adequate access to medical attention and counselling while in government custody;

•   release children as promptly as possible to their families or to appropriate child welfare organizations, rather than holding the children for questioning in military barracks;

•   ensure that an adequate number of trained counselors exists to work with the children, with special attention paid to the needs of girls who have been sexually abused;

•   promptly reunite children with family members;

•   initiate a widespread information and education campaign to inform communities of the special needs of children who were abducted;

•   facilitate the children's full and speedy reintegration into their communities;

•   develop a concrete plan for meeting the long-term needs of the children;

•   ensure that government soldiers respect the human rights of civilians in the north;

•   ensure that people living in government-established "protected camps" have adequate food, water, sanitation, and health care, and are protected from rebel attacks.

To the United Nations

•   the U.N.'s special rapporteur for Sudan should investigate and report on the role of Sudan in supporting the Lord's Resistance Army, with special attention to the LRA's abduction, killing, torture and sexual abuse of children;

• the U.N. Secretary General's special representative on the impact of armed conflict on children should promptly investigate the abduction, killing, torture and sexual abuse of children by the Lord's Resistance Army;

• the U.N. Secretary General should request that the U.N. High Commissioner for Refugees (UNHCR) work with Ugandans who have been internally displaced because of the conflict in the north, to help ensure that displaced persons, and especially children, have access to adequate food, water, health care and sanitary facilities;

• the U.N. Committee on the Rights of the Child should conduct an on-site investigation into the situation of children held in captivity by the Lord's Resistance Army, and into the situation of children who have escaped from the LRA and returned to Uganda;

• UNICEF should monitor conditions for children in trauma counseling centers and protected camps, and work with the government, NGOs and relief agencies to improve conditions;

• the U.N. Working Group on a Draft Optional Protocol to the Convention on the Rights of the Child on Involvement of Children in Armed Conflicts should uncompromisingly seek to raise to eighteen the minimum age at which people may be recruited into armed forces and participate in hostilities (whether that recruitment is voluntary or compulsory, and whether it is into governmental or nongovernmental armed forces). African states should be encouraged to participate actively in the working group.

To the international community

• urge the Ugandan government to take all possible steps to minimize child casualties during fighting with the Lord's Resistance Army;

• press the Sudanese government to use its influence to stop the Lord's Resistance Army from abducting, killing, torturing and sexually abusing children, and to discontinue all Sudanese aid to the Lord's Resistance Army until it complies with the recommendations outlined above.

• actively support the efforts of the U.N. Working Group on the Draft Optional Protocol to the Convention on the Rights of the Child to raise to eighteen the minimum age for recruitment into armed forces and participation in hostilities.

To the Organization of African Unity

• the African Commission on Human and Peoples' Rights should investigate and report on human rights abuses by the Lord's Resistance Army.

II. THE ABDUCTION OF CHILDREN BY
THE LORD'S RESISTANCE ARMY

Background

The origin of the current conflict lies in the complex religious traditions of the Acholi people who inhabit Uganda's northernmost districts, and in the deeply-rooted ethnic mistrust between the Acholi and the ethnic groups of southern Uganda—a mistrust that has often erupted into widespread violence.

During the period of British colonial administration, the British employed mostly southerners in the civil service; people from northern Uganda, and especially the Acholi, were primarily recruited into the armed forces. This created a division between northern and southern Uganda that persisted through independence in 1962: the south was more developed and contained the bulk of Uganda's educated elite, while the north, including Gulu and Kitgum, the homeland of the Acholi, was much poorer, with the people relying on cattle and military service for subsistence.

The socio-economic division between north and south has been exacerbated by frequent bouts of ethnic violence. According to most historians of post-independence Uganda, Acholi soldiers have been both victims and perpetrators of this violence. Under Milton Obote's first presidency, Acholi soldiers were implicated in many of the government's questionable activities. In the 1970s, during the administration of the notorious Idi Amin, many Acholi soldiers were slaughtered by Amin's henchmen. After Amin's 1979 overthrow, Milton Obote returned to power, and the Acholi soldiers in his army were implicated in the deaths of thousands of civilians during the civil war against Yoweri Museveni's guerrilla National Resistance Army, which drew its support mostly from people in Uganda's southern and western regions.[1]

Museveni's eventual military victory was preceded by a brief period of Acholi control of the government, when Acholi army officer Tito Okello ousted Milton Obote. After Okello's coup, Okello entered into peace talks with Museveni's still-hostile National Resistance Army, and after several months, the

---

[1]See Thomas P. Ofcansky, *Uganda: Tarnished Pearl of Africa* (Boulder: Westview Press, 1996), Chapter 3, *passim*; A.B.K. Kasozi, *The Social Origins of Violence in Uganda*, 1964-1985 (Montreal: McGill-Queens University Press, 1994), pp. 11, 54; Amii Omara-Otunnu, *Politics and the Military in Uganda*, 1980-1985 (London: Macmillan, 1987), pp. 104, 125-126, 158-159.

Nairobi Peace Accord was signed by the two parties. But the peace accord was never implemented, because fighting broke out a mere two weeks after it was signed, with each side accusing the other of having breached the agreement. On January 26, 1986, Museveni's National Resistance Army took Kampala.[2]

Okello's Acholi soldiers retreated north. Some crossed the border and took refuge with the Acholi people of southern Sudan, but many retreated only as far as Gulu and Kitgum, where they could rely on the support of the civilian population. Nonetheless, the National Resistance Army soon succeeded in taking the major northern towns, and it appeared that Museveni was firmly in control of all of Uganda. Acholi ex-soldiers were asked to turn in their weapons, and many did so.

Some, however, never relinquished their weapons. According to Paulinus Nyeko, chairman of Gulu Human Rights Focus, since Uganda's history for twenty-five years had been one of ethnic purges and reprisals, many Acholi feared that it was only a matter of time before Museveni's soldiers sought revenge on them for atrocities committed during past regimes.[3] And the behavior of many of the National Resistance Army soldiers did little to quell these fears. Harassment, looting, rape and cattle-theft by National Resistance Army soldiers were not infrequent, and did little to increase Acholi faith in the new Museveni government.[4]

By August 1987, many of the Acholi ex-soldiers in Sudan had joined up with other opponents of the Museveni administration, and formed a rebel alliance. The rebels made frequent incursions into Uganda to fight the government's National Resistance Army. (The NRA was later rechristened the Uganda People's Defense Force, or UPDF.)

One of the rebel units, the Holy Spirit Mobile Force, was led by self-styled Acholi prophetess Alice Lakwena. She claimed to be possessed by the Holy Spirit, and garnered enormous Acholi support with her promises to defeat Museveni's government and purge the Acholi people of witches and sinners. (The fourth section of this report discusses the emergence of Alice Lakwena's Holy Spirit movement in greater detail).

---

[2] Ofcansky, *Uganda*, pp. 56-58.

[3] Human Rights Watch interview, Gulu, May 30, 1997.

[4] Museveni and other senior officials have acknowledged human rights violations by NRA forces during this period, and tried and punished some of the soldiers involved. The Parliament of Uganda, "Report of the Committee on Defense and Internal Affairs on the War in Northern Uganda," January 1997, pp. 11-12.

In late 1987, Alice Lakwena led thousands of Acholi soldiers against government troops; her soldiers were anointed with shea butter oil, which Lakwena assured them would cause bullets to bounce harmlessly off their chests. Aided by the civilian population, Lakwena's Holy Spirit Mobile Force soldiers got to within sixty miles of Kampala, where they encountered a large government force. Lakwena's soldiers, armed largely with rifles and stones, proved to be no match for modern heavy artillery, and thousands of her followers were killed. Lakwena herself fled to Kenya.

In the wake of Lakwena's defeat, the Acholi rebel movement disintegrated and many Acholi rebels surrendered. But a few remained in the bush, under the leadership of Joseph Kony, a young relative of Lakwena's. Kony claimed to be the inheritor of Lakwena's spiritual tradition, and his small group of rebels, based in Sudan, eventually came to call itself the Lord's Resistance Army. Like Alice Lakwena, Kony promised both to overthrow the northern-dominated government and to purify the Acholi people from within—and both these goals were to be accomplished through violence.

Despite years of government attempts to stamp it out, the Lord's Resistance Army (often called the "Kony rebels" by Ugandans) persists, never strong enough to seriously destabilize the government, but never weak enough to die out completely. Sudanese government spokesmen have repeatedly accused the Ugandan government of providing military support to the rebel Sudanese People's Liberation Army (SPLA), and several years ago, in apparent retaliation, the Sudanese government began to aid the Lord's Resistance Army.[5] According to the many children interviewed by Human Rights Watch, the Sudanese government also relies on the Lord's Resistance Army to help fight the SPLA. Sudanese government aid has turned the Lord's Resistance Army into more of a threat than ever, since the rebels are now armed with land mines and machine guns in place of rifles and machetes.

The recent activities of the Lord's Resistance Army have turned Gulu and Kitgum into permanent battle zones, filled with burnt schools, ransacked homes, abandoned fields, and a huge population of internally displaced people. One of the many tragic aspects of the conflict is that it is mostly Acholi civilians who are

---

[5] For a brief discussion of Sudan's charges against Uganda and the Ugandan government response, see, for instance, Nhial Bol, "Sudan-Uganda: Khartoum Denies Air Attack on Ugandan Town," Interpress Service, February 16, 1997.

dying as a result of the activities of the rebels, the vast majority of whom are Acholi themselves. But it is the region's children who have suffered the most.[6]

The Children's Stories

The children of northern Uganda are the victims of atrocious human rights violations of a severity that is difficult to imagine, and the actions of the Lord's Resistance Army violate the most basic principles both of customary international law and of human morality.[7]

This report is based on research conducted in Uganda in late May and early June of 1997. In addition to holding background interviews with representatives of the government, the military and the NGO community, we interviewed about thirty children who had escaped from rebel captivity.[8] Most of the children we interviewed were between the ages of ten and seventeen. Some of our interviews were conducted in English, but the majority were conducted with the aid of interpreters. We also collected written testimonials (in English) from over a hundred schoolgirls who had been abducted *en masse* from St. Mary's school in the town of Aboke in October of 1996.[9]

---

[6] In this report, the word "children" refers to anyone under the age of eighteen. The U.N. Convention on the Rights of the Child defines a child as "every human being under the age of eighteen unless, under the law applicable to the child, majority is obtained earlier." Article 1. Convention on the Rights of the Child, G.A. res. 44/25, annex 44 U.N. GAOR Supp. (No 49), at 167, U.N. Doc. A/4/49 (1989). The full text of the Convention on the Rights of the Child is set forth in the Appendix.

[7] Our findings in this report are corroborated by the findings of a team of Amnesty International researchers, which visited Uganda in May 1997. See Amnesty International, *Breaking God's Commands: The Destruction of Childhood by the Lord's Resistance Army in Uganda*, AI Index: AFR 59/01/97 (London: September 18, 1997). See also UNICEF/ World Vision, *Shattered Innocence: Testimonies of Children Abducted in Northern Uganda*, (Uganda:1997).

[8] It should be noted that the children we interviewed are somewhat atypical, in that they succeeded in escaping from the rebels, something most abducted children never do. In our investigation, we had to rely solely on the testimony of those children who had escaped from the rebels, since it is impossible to gain access to the rebel camps and interview children still in captivity.

[9] A number of these testimonials are included in the appendix to this report.

Words like "brutal" and "egregious" appear frequently in the reports of human rights groups. Although such terms are used with care and justification, at some point they lose their power to move us: the litany of violations becomes numbing, rather than shocking. For that reason, the first part of this report will be almost entirely in the children's own words. The second section of the report will discuss the indirect effects of the conflict, while the third section will provide a more in-depth discussion of the history and causes of the violence that is devastating northern Uganda.

The following excerpts from the children's stories have been lightly edited for clarity, but are otherwise unchanged. Ages given are ages of the children at the time of our interviews in May 1997. Most of the children we met had been held by the rebels for months and sometimes several years before managing to escape.

To protect the children, we have changed all names and altered other identifying characteristics.

Capture and Early Days

Typically, the rebels appear to divide into small bands in order to lead raids into Uganda. Groups of five to twenty rebels wander through the bush, maintaining radio contact with their fellows. In towns, the rebels loot trading posts and steal medicines from small health clinics. In the bush, they loot compounds, beating and often killing the adults, and abducting many of the children. They burn huts when they leave, and steal everything edible or useful. The small rebel bands then reunite, and march together back across the Sudanese border.

Abducted children are generally tied up and forced to carry looted goods. Unused to long marches through the bush, most of the children soon develop swollen and infected feet. Despite the constant looting of stores and homes, the rebels often have only limited food supplies, and new captives receive little to eat. The children are frequently beaten for little or no reason.

Weak with hunger, sore from constant beatings, and limping on infected feet, many of the children have trouble keeping up with the group. But children who cannot keep up are killed, and those children who try to escape face brutal repercussions: the rebels force other new captives to help beat or stab to death unsuccessful escapees. For those children who survive, taking part in the murder of other captives forms a gruesome initiation into the ways of the Lord's Resistance Army.

Charles, fifteen:

> There had already been rumors that rebels were around, and we
> were very fearful. My grandmother was hiding in the bush. It
> was morning, and I was practicing my music when I heard a
> shot. I started running into the bush, but there was a rebel hiding
> behind a tree. I thought he would shoot me. He said, "Stop, my
> friend, don't try to run away!" Then he beat me with the handle
> of the gun on my back. He ordered me to direct him, and told
> me that afterwards I would be released.
>
> But afterwards it was quite different. That afternoon we met
> with a very huge group of rebels, together with so many new
> captives. We marched and marched. In the bush we came
> across three young boys who had escaped from the rebels earlier,
> and they removed the boys' shirts and tied ropes around their
> throats, so that when they killed them they would make no noise.
> Then they forced them down and started clubbing their heads,
> and other rebels came with bayonets and stabbed them. It was
> not a good sight.

Thomas, fourteen:

> In our village, we realized the rebels were coming, and my
> whole family hid in the bush at night. At dawn, we thought they
> were gone, and I went back to the compound to fetch food. But
> they were still there, and they took me. It was very fast. The
> rest of my family was still in hiding. The rebels had already
> abducted about a hundred children, and they had looted a lot of
> foodstuff. But they would just give you only very little food to
> keep you going.
>
> I had to carry a bag of groundnuts, maybe twenty kilos. It was
> heavy but there was no alternative to carrying it. Some young
> children were given very heavy loads, but with any load you
> must struggle to carry it, or otherwise the rebels say, "You are
> becoming stubborn and rebellious!" And they kill you. If your
> feet swell they also kill you.

> I saw quite a number of children killed. Most of them were killed with clubs. They would take five or six of the newly abducted children and make them kill those who had fallen or tried to escape. It was so painful to watch. Twice I had to help. And to do it, it was so bad, it was very bad to have to do.

Stephen, seventeen:

> I was abducted twice. The first time I escaped. It was not safe in my village so I came to the town, but after a while I decided to go back to the village and collect my property. But while I was there I was again abducted. Luckily it was a different group and they did not recognize me, or they would have killed me.

> They cut me with a panga (machete) and tied me and they said that if I had money, I must give it to them. I said, "Where can I get money? I am just a schoolboy." So they beat me and beat me. They took all the food in our house, and they took the bicycle my uncle gave me to ride to school and cut it up with an ax.[10] They beat all my young cousins who were just small boys, four or five years old. One of them they killed. Then they burned the house.

The youngest child we interviewed was ten-year-old William. He trembled throughout the interview, and clung to the interviewer's hand. As he spoke, his voice got softer and softer, and his head bowed down until his forehead rested on the table.

William, ten:

> It was at seven p.m. We were in the house, and two of us were abducted. It was me and my older brother. My mother was

---

[10] The rebels destroy bicycles (and often kill or mutilate their owners) because the bicycle is a relatively quick form of transportation over poorly maintained rural roads. The rebels fear that the existence of bicycles enables civilians to warn government soldiers quickly of rebel activity.

crying and they beat her. She was weakly and I do not know if she is all right at all.

They beat us, then they made me carry some radios and carry the commander's gun. It was heavy and at first I was afraid it would shoot off in my arms, but it was not filled with ammunition. We joined a big group and we walked very far, and my feet were very swollen. If you said that you were hurting they would say, "Shall we give this young boy a rest?" But by a "rest" they meant they would kill you, so if you did not wish to die you had to say you did not need a rest.

Many children tried to escape and were killed. They made us help. I was afraid and I missed my mother. But my brother was very strong-hearted and he told me we must have courage, we will not die, so I kept going.

After the interview, William went and sat by himself on a patch of grass near our interview table. One of the counselors, looking at him, sighed: "This one, he is needing a lot of love."

On paper, the children's stories have a terrible sameness: "The rebels took me, they made me march, I was afraid, my feet swelled, I had to help kill another child . . . ." But for all their similarities, the stories are each unique: one child recalls a visit from the spirit of his dead brother; another remembers the chicken the rebels forced him to pluck more quickly than he was able; a third remembers the blood that dripped from the mouth of a child being clubbed to death.

James, fourteen:

Me and my brothers and cousins were playing football. Five rebels came and took all six of us, my three brothers, two cousins and myself. They tied us with ropes around our waists and gave us heavy loads to carry. [They led us to a larger group.] There were about eighty rebels and fifty abductees in the group. At night, we stopped to rest, and they beat us—they used a bicycle chain to beat us. The next morning we came to the government soldiers when we were walking. They were firing at us. We ran with the luggage.

My eldest brother escaped but the rebels caught him and they killed him. They beat him on the back of the head with a club. I watched him being killed. His *tipu* (spirit) came to me and covered me and told me, "Today, I am dead."

I was in shock . . . . My other two brothers and I were allowed to stay together but we were told that if any of us escaped, one of us would be killed.

George, fourteen:

It was around ten a.m. and my two brothers and I were doing handicrafts. The rebels appeared all of a sudden. They had guns. They took all three of us, and they ordered us to remove our shirts and run with their group. We ran for about five miles, and came to a larger group, and they gave us chickens and ordered us to remove their feathers very fast. I was not good enough and they beat me with their guns to make me hurry. As we prepared their meal we were attacked by government forces. I was shot in the arm but I still had to march. They killed you if you could not march.

Stella, fifteen:

They came to our school in the middle of the night. We were hiding under the beds but they banged on the beds and told us to come out. They tied us and led us out, and they tried to set the school building on fire. We walked and walked and they made us carry their property that they had looted. At about six a. m. they made us stop and they lined up in two lines, and made us walk between them while they kicked us.

On the second day of marching our legs were swollen. They said, "Eh, now, what should we do about your legs? You must walk, or do you want us to kill you? It's your choice." So we kept going.

On the third day a little girl tried to escape, and they made us kill her. They went to collect some big pieces of firewood. Then they kicked her and jumped on her, and they made us each beat her at least once with the big pieces of wood. They said, "You must beat and beat and beat her." She was bleeding from the mouth. Then she died. Then they made us lie down and they beat us with fifteen strokes each, because they said we had known she would try to escape.

Many of the children spoke of being so frightened and bewildered that nothing seemed real anymore. The pain, fear, and shock combine to create a numbness, a dizziness—a sense, at times, that madness is not far off.

Sharon, thirteen:

I was abducted while my mother and I were going to the field . . . . One of the other abducted girls tried to escape but she was caught. The rebels told us that she had tried to escape and must be killed. They made the new children kill her. They told us that if we escaped, they would kill our families.

They made us walk for a week . . . . Some of the smaller children could not keep up, as we were walking so far without resting, and they were killed . . . . Some of the children died of hunger. I felt lifeless seeing so many children dying and being killed. I thought I would be killed.

Samuel, seventeen:

About thirteen rebels came and took me and my brothers from our home. It was at night and I was sleeping. The rebels made us take off our shirts and tied our hands behind our backs. We began walking and met up with other rebels and children who had been abducted. They untied our hands and tied us by the waist to the other children.

Many people were killed because they could not walk further. They were stabbed with bayonets in their chests and heads. It was so horrible, I felt that I was going crazy. I felt dizzy a lot, my head spinning most of the time.

Christine, seventeen:

> It was around two or three a.m. I woke to the sound of windows breaking, and torches flashing. I don't know how many rebels there were. Some of us were beaten. I was shaking . . . . We walked the whole night, through the bush and on small paths. While we were walking, they would kick us or slap us, or hit us with gun butts, and sometime with sticks.
>
> Whenever they killed anyone, they called us to watch. I saw eleven people killed this way. One of them was a boy who had escaped. They found him in his home, and called him outside. They made him lie down on the ground, and they pierced him with a bayonet. They chopped him with the bayonet until he was dead. Seeing this, at times, I felt like I was a dead person—not feeling anything. And then sometimes I would feel like it was happening to me, and I would feel the pain.

Phillip, fourteen:

> I saw my older brother go mad . . . He would be given food and would just throw it on the ground, and mix it with dirt and eat it. I was allowed to talk with him, and he would tell me about how our mother was here and our sister. He thought that we were at home. I don't know what happened to him. We saw so many people killed, bodies sticking out of trenches, and gun shots all around. It was so frightening. Maybe that made him mad.

On the March in Uganda and Sudan

After abduction, some children remain in the bush in Uganda for several months, used by the rebels as porters and servants. At some point, however, most children who have not escaped or been killed are brought across the border into Sudan, where the rebels have their main base. In southern Sudan as in Uganda, the rebels loot homes and trading centers, spreading carnage and destruction wherever they go.

Charles, fifteen:

> After my abduction, we marched and marched. Once we passed close to my homestead, but I was carefully guarded and I could do nothing. We came across a car which we ambushed, and later we came to a homestead and found a family with a father who was drunk. The rebels said, "This one is drunk, we cannot spare him!" So they clubbed him to death, then dragged him to a hut and burned it. As we went we burned many houses. I also recall that after we attacked a Kitgum trading center, we came across two hunters, and they were killed with clubs and bayonets.
>
> This looting and killing continued as we marched. So many people were killed. You had to adapt yourself quickly to that kind of life.

James, fourteen:

> Every day, each rebel had to get abductees. Our team's major work was to abduct other children. They would have contests to see who could get the most captives. We worked a lot. The abductees were made to dig, making granaries. They told us we were fighting to overthrow the government, but we didn't do fighting. When we saw government soldiers, we just ran.

Timothy, fourteen:

> We walked very long distances. All I could think about was home and being with my family. Sometimes there were helicopter attacks [by government forces]. I was injured: my skin and my chest and arms were burned during an attack. Many children were killed, and others lost legs from bombs.

Marching, looting, marching, looting, killing. For many children, the clearest memories from this period are of the exhaustion and the apparently aimless marching. And, of course, of the atrocities they witnessed and were forced to take part in.

Teddy, thirteen:

> We walked for a very long distance, day and night, and we slept
> with no food given to us. As we moved we crossed the river
> between Gulu and Kitgum. The water almost killed us, because
> we could not swim. We crossed a main road and came across
> five people riding bicycles, and the rebels killed them because
> bicycles are against their rules: the rebels fear fast delivery of
> information about their presence. They would send young
> children to climb trees for observation, but still we were often
> attacked by government soldiers, and many were killed. I was
> shot in the leg, but it missed the bone and afterwards I recovered.
>
> After one battle where many rebels were killed we spent a long
> time deep in the bush, far from villages. After a time we came
> to a camp for rebels who had been wounded or were sick. This
> was still in Uganda. My duty was to go look for food. Often we
> stole it. Another of my assignments was to wash the clothes of
> the wounded and sick. They were dirty clothes, covered with
> blood and stains, and I also had to clean out gumboots that had
> filled with blood.
>
> When I had been with the rebels for some weeks they learned
> that I had not given them my own name, Teddy, but had told
> them my name was different. They learned this because of a bad
> coincidence: we met with another group of rebels as we
> marched, and one of the boys in the other group was from my
> village. He recognized me and called me by my name. So the
> commander of my group was angry, and said "Why did you
> deceive me?" He said he would kill me and they began to
> prepare for my death.
>
> When they want to kill somebody they start with prayers for
> your soul. They even started praying for me. But the
> commander of the other rebel group pleaded for me, and said,
> "Do not kill this young boy. Instead let him join us in our
> struggle."

Catherine, seventeen:

> We would walk through villages where the civilians had fled . .
> . we would sleep in deserted villages, and eat and stay in the
> houses. Sometimes there were villagers who had stayed behind
> . . . the rebels would accuse them [of supporting the
> government]. One day, they found a man riding a bike. They
> just cut off his foot with an ax. When his wife came out of the
> house, they told her to eat the foot. I turned away not to see
> what happened.

Christine, seventeen:

> They told us we were soldiers now, we were no longer students.
> We were walking always, day and night. I don't know where
> we were going. Sometimes I found that we were walking in
> circles—we would pass a spot that I recognized from before.
> As far as I know, their work was to walk around, but they had no
> place to stay. Sometimes we slept in houses, in the same houses
> with civilians. The rebels would ask the villagers if the
> government soldiers were around. The civilians would tell
> them. They made us carry clothes, and food for cooking. We
> had to cook for ourselves—they would give us food to cook for
> ourselves. Sometimes there was not time to eat.
>
> [Sometimes] they beat us, fifteen strokes each. When they beat
> you, they tell you not to touch the areas where we were beaten.
> I touched myself there, and so did another girl. For that they
> made us step out and lie down on the ground. Then they beat
> us with canes. There were seven of them.

Patricia, fifteen:

> They made us walk for a week. Some of the children were
> young and not used to walking, but if you sit down to rest, they
> beat you, and sometimes they just shoot you . . . . I saw so many
> children dying. About fifty children in my group died. I was so
> scared. I didn't know where we were going.

They would make us cut people's legs off. If you don't help they beat you. My back still hurt from the beatings. But I would not help. They said, "We will kill you some day, you are misbehaving!" I said, "If you kill me, I will become a saint."

When we reached the Sudan border and I saw the Arab people I knew I was in Sudan. In Sudan, so many children died of diarrhea and hunger.

In southern Sudan, a severe draught makes survival difficult, and during long marches through the bush, water is often scarce or non-existent. Food, too, is limited, and when it cannot be looted from villages, the children are reduced to foraging for wild leaves. Many children die of hunger, thirst, or dysentery before ever reaching the Sudanese camp.

Charles, fifteen:

After a time we received a radio message to go to Sudan to meet Joseph Kony's group. We started marching and it became very dry. We could not find water or food, and we ate the leaves of trees. Many became sick and died, and you would see children everywhere, lying down like they were sleeping. But they were dead.

Susan, sixteen:

I spent three months in Uganda and three months in Sudan with the rebels. In Uganda, we were made to do a lot of hard work—getting rice, pounding rice, hulling rice, stealing food, and gathering wild leaves and preparing food. We were always hungry. There was never enough food. Most people in the villages we passed through had run away.

On the way to Sudan we passed so many dead bodies of people who had died along the way—people who died of hunger, or sickness, or were killed.

Samuel, seventeen:

> It was so hot. It was the dry season and I had blisters on my feet
> from walking so much. They never told us where we were going
> or why we had been taken. We were given raw food, simsim
> and boiled sorghum to eat, but no water. The water ran out after
> two days, and many people died of thirst. We walked for three
> days straight, without sleeping, until we reached Sudan. In
> Sudan, the main problems were diseases: dysentery and
> malaria—and food shortages and not enough water.

Life in the Rebel Camps in Sudan

The rebels have at least one major camp in southern Sudan. Kony, the
Lord's Resistance Army leader, lives in the camp along with his top commanders.
There may at one time have been many more Lord's Resistance Army camps, but
some were recently destroyed by the rebel Sudanese People's Liberation Army,
which has friendly ties to the Ugandan government.

In the camp in Sudan, the children (both boys and girls) are trained to use
weapons and fight. The weapons are supplied by the Sudanese government;
children report the frequent arrival of heavy lorries containing weapons and
supplies, driven by soldiers in Sudanese army uniforms.

We heard repeated allegations that in Sudan, some Ugandan children were
sold as slaves to the Sudanese, in exchange for guns and food. We were unable to
obtain any direct confirmation of these rumors, but the possibility cannot be
discounted.[11]

Thomas, fourteen:

> In Sudan, they brought us to a large camp. There were maybe
> 5,000 people there. My duties were mostly to farm. I would dig
> fields and plant maize beans. I spent most of my time digging.
> They also trained us in how to be soldiers. I was trained to use
> mortars, RPG, and SMG weapons. The guns came from the
> Arabs and the Sudanese government. Kony had lorries that were

---

[11] The existence of slavery in Sudan (particularly involving children from southern
Sudan) has been well-documented. See, for instance, Human Rights Watch/Africa &
Human Rights Watch Children's Rights Project, *Children of Sudan: Slaves, Street Children
and Child Soldiers* (New York: Human Rights Watch, 1995).

given him by the Sudan government. They would leave the camp and come back, loaded with guns.

Sharon, thirteen:

> When we got to Sudan, I saw some children there that I knew from my village. They had also been abducted earlier. Our group was divided into four smaller groups of about a hundred people. I was the youngest in my group. I was twelve. Others were about thirteen or fourteen years old. They trained us in how to use guns, and the names of all the gun parts. The camp in Sudan was large. There were about a thousand people there. I stayed there for three months. Most of the time I was just made to work—like digging for potatoes.

Timothy, fourteen:

> After we crossed into Sudan, we went to a place called Kit where they trained us. Kony told us we would go back to Uganda and overthrow the government—we were trained how to attack vehicles, and how to shoot.

> Kony would tell us that we would overthrow the government. People should be happy and wait for that day to come. He also warned us that if we were caught becoming friendly with any girl, we would be killed together—the boy and the girl. He also warned us that if we tried to escape we would be killed.

> After my training, I was given a gun: an AK47. I had to carry it on my right shoulder at all times. It was so heavy. The loaded magazine made it so heavy. For a while, my right arm was paralyzed from the weight, and the skin on my shoulder burned from carrying it. I had chest pains. I was also given things to carry like cans of water.

Mary, fifteen:

> In Kony's camp we saw things like weapons and guns, all types of guns and ammunition. I think they came from Khartoum.

We all underwent training, every day, training in how to operate
the guns, and how to name them. Sometimes we would have to
jog with our guns and sing soldier songs, and also prayer songs.
Then we would go home and cook the vine leaves. Children
tried always to escape, but some of them were recaptured and
killed.

Sarah, sixteen:

In Sudan they gave us training for three weeks. Kony sent a
message to send the young ones to him in Palataka. Kony
wanted those who had been in schools to be trained as nurses, to
give first aid to the rebels. I was one of those. But I was also
trained to shoot, and how to put together guns and handle the
weapons—antipersonnel mines, antitank mines, SMG, LMF,
PKM, mortars. The weapons were brought by Arabs in
uniforms.

Samuel, seventeen:

In Sudan, we were informed that we were now soldiers. They
said we would be given one week to rest, and then we would be
begin military training. I went through three weeks of military
training. We were given guns and were selected to fight in
Sudan. There were confrontations between the Lord's
Resistance Army and the UPDF in Sudan. The weapons we
used [included] mortars and antipersonnel land mines. The BKs
were the preferred weapon among us—it was the most reliable.
It takes two people to operate it: one person to hold and feed the
chain of bullets, and the other to shoot.

Kony abducts children for military purposes. The children are
trained to make soldiers. Other children are taken to be
wives—the girls. Others are taken to be porters, to carry things.
There are also some who are brought to be killed in front of the
new recruits, to build courage. In Sudan, some men were
brought before us, and we were made to gather in a circle. We
had to beat the man to death. The real killing was done by
about ten people, and the rest were made to beat the person who

was already dead. The new recruits are made to do this to build courage.

Although conditions in the camp are somewhat better than conditions on the march, many children still spoke of being hungry and thirsty all the time. The best food is reserved for the rebel commanders, and child captives often have to supplement their meager rations with wild leaves. Deaths from malnutrition and disease continue.

Jessica, fourteen:

> There was no water in the camp. Every day we would have to go search for water. The Arabs brought food and guns from Juba, and the food was mostly beans, but it was not enough. We ate bitter leaves. People were dying, especially young boys. There were many boys of about seven years of age who had been abducted from Gulu, and they were many of them dying.
>
> There were more than a thousand people in the camp at the time I was there. Most rebels were young children who had been captured like me, but there were many who were very old, forty or older. Kony himself is about thirty or thirty-five years old. He had eighteen women for himself, and six children had been born to him.

Patricia, fifteen:

> In Sudan, so many children died of diarrhea and hunger . . . . We were given food, but very little—maybe a little bread and beans. They would give us food maybe once a month—the food was brought by the Arabs. During the days, I would go out looking for food. Sometimes we would be beaten if we came back without finding any food. There was no water. You had to walk miles to collect water. At night, I slept in an *adaki* [trench].

Phillip, fourteen:

> There was very little food in Sudan. Ten people would be fed
> from one small bowl. I was always hungry.
>
> I was made to beat two boys who took too long to get water.
> They were little boys.
>
> I was given a sub-machine gun and had to carry it with me at all
> times: when you're going to get water, or to collect firewood,
> you still have to carry it. It was very heavy for me.

Stephen, seventeen:

> When we were in the Sudan there, we were not feeling well at
> all.   There was lack of food and no medicines, and we were
> feeling very, very, very bad, and not okay at all.
>
> In the Sudan, some people were dying of hunger, and diarrhea
> was also very serious. But should you make a mistake of
> stealing things, you will be tied to a tree and shot by a firing
> squad. These very young children especially, they very much
> miss the food they used to have at home. But if you take food
> they just shoot you, even the very young ones. Death only is the
> punishment for this.

For girls, life in Sudan is particularly hard. In addition to military
training, farming, and cooking, most girls who have hit puberty have an additional
duty: they are given to rebel commanders as "wives." Although the Lord's
Resistance Army has strict rules against voluntary sexual relationships between
captives, girls given as wives to commanders are forced to provide sexual services;
those who refuse are often beaten until they comply.

Theresa, eighteen:

> I was made to be wife to three men. Three rebels were fighting
> over me and each one wanted me to be his wife. One of them
> wanted to kill me. He took me as his wife, and I did not want to
> be his wife. He said if I refused he would kill me, and if I ran

away he would kill me. He was sent away to fight, and then I was made to be wife to a second man. Then he also was sent away to fight, and I was given to a third man. The third man was a big leader, and when he went away to fight he wanted me to go with him.

Susan, sixteen:

One week after I was abducted I was given to a man called Abonga. He was thirty years old. Two girls were given to him. He was trying to be nice to me, to make me feel happy and not want to run away, but all I wanted to do was go home. I was taken away from him when I got to Sudan because I had syphilis. They said they wanted to give me treatment, but I refused—I did not trust them and thought that they might try to hurt me, and I felt fine anyway. Because I had syphilis, I was not given to another man in Sudan. Instead I was kept separately and guarded because they thought I would give the sickness to others.

No one was allowed to have free relationships there. If they caught a boy and a girl together they would shoot you in public. The only relationships they allowed were the ones that they forced on you.

Catherine, seventeen:

They gave us all as wives. I think four of the girls abducted from the St. Mary School at Aboke were given to Kony as wives; they stayed with Kony's other girls. They gave me as a wife, but I refused the man. The soldier I was given to already had a girl who was five months pregnant. He ordered other boys to beat me on my back with a panga. He hated me. I got eight strokes with the panga on my back. It hurt so much, I thought I would die. After that we never spoke. I just stayed with the other girls.

Sarah, seventeen:

> After the military training, I was given to a man called Otim.
> There were five women given to one man. The man I was given
> to was very rude to me: he thought I wanted to leave him and
> escape. He beat me many times with sticks. He thought I
> wanted to escape. Now I'm going to be a mother soon.
>
> I don't want to be a mother at this age. But it happened and I
> must accept this.

Religion and Ideology
The children we interviewed had only the haziest idea why the rebels were
fighting: "They want to overthrow the government" was a refrain we heard
repeatedly, but few children, regardless of how long they had been with the rebels,
were able to articulate anything specific about the rebels' program.

Thomas, fourteen:

> Joseph Kony came out to address us several times. He said the
> present president of Uganda is biased and is only developing the
> west and south, and is neglecting development in the north, but
> that he, Kony, would develop the north. He always would warn
> the abductees not to escape. He would tell us to be patient, and
> we would overthrow the government, so be patient and wait.

Catherine, seventeen:

> When we tried to ask them questions, they said they capture
> people because they want to disappoint Museveni, and to break
> the government. I don't know how they'll ever do that. They
> will never overthrow the government.

Stephen, seventeen:

> The rebels say that they don't want this man Museveni who is
> ruling Uganda, because he has killed a lot of Acholi, he has
> killed a lot of their brothers, mothers, fathers, aunts and sisters.
> So they don't want this man who is ruling, and they want to take

the government from him. Museveni caused a lot of Acholi life to be lost, and therefore he can never rule Acholiland, and the rebels say they will fight until the government falls down and the Acholi are rich in Uganda.

Mary, fifteen:

> Kony was talking of the overthrow of the government and was prophesizing that the government would soon come to an end. He said it was wrong that Museveni was ruling over the Acholi. "Let him go rule his own people in the south and west," he said, "But we will not let him rule in Acholiland."

Western news reports tend to depict Joseph Kony's Lord's Resistance Army as a group of violent Christian fundamentalists, committed to establishing a government based upon the Ten Commandments.   This is a misleading oversimplification, however. Kony was brought up partially in the Catholic tradition, and claims to be doing the bidding of the Holy Spirit, but in practice the rebels perform an eclectic mix of rituals, some drawn from Christianity, some from the indigenous Acholi tribal religion, and, increasingly, some from Islam.

Molly, seventeen:

> They prayed a lot, but they didn't pray like normal Christians. Sometimes they would use rosaries, but sometimes they would bow down like Muslims. They said they had a *malaika* [spirit, angel]. They said the malaika said there would be a terrible fight, and that the government would be overthrown. After that, they said, we would be released. Sometimes they would gather us together and try to convince us to believe them.

> They believed in their local gods, and they didn't want us to learn about their malaika. They discouraged us from asking questions about them or their beliefs. If you asked too many questions they would become cruel.

Christine, seventeen:

> The rebels call Joseph Kony their father, and say that the Holy
> Spirit speaks to him, and tells him what to do. But I don't see
> anything to their religion.   At times they pray like they're
> Christians, and at times like they're Muslims.   They made us
> kneel and face in one direction to pray, like Muslims.   Their
> customs are strange. If they've just abducted you, they smear
> you with oil in the sign of the cross, on your forehead and on
> your chest. They did that to us on the third day after we were
> abducted. They said it was their custom. Another one of their
> customs is they don't eat with strangers.
>
> After we had been with them for three weeks, they drew a
> picture of a large heart in the ground, and divided it into thirty
> squares. They told us to bathe and to remove our blouses and
> remain bare-chested. They told each of us to stand in one of the
> squares. They dipped an egg in a mixture of white powder and
> water, and drew a heart on our chests and our backs. They also
> made a sign of the cross on our foreheads and on our across our
> lips. Then they poured water on us. The commander, Lagira,
> told us to stay without our blouses for three days. He said what
> they were doing was written in the bible. Another man told us
> they were doing this for our protection.
>
> They said they were preparing to overthrow the government, and
> that the day for the fight would take place if a child between ten
> and fifteen years old would have a certain dream about them, or
> if someone would rise at dawn and see a hand in the
> clouds—that would mean that there were five days before the
> fight. But this would happen, and then time would pass, and
> nothing happened. They didn't overthrow the government.

Stella, fifteen:

> Sometimes they behaved like Muslims, sometimes like
> Catholics, sometimes like Protestants. They said they would
> overthrow the government within three years. They said they
> wanted Uganda to become a paradise. I said, "If you want a

paradise, why are you killing people in Northern Uganda? The government is down south in Kampala, so how can you expect to overthrow the government if you kill people here?"

They said, "Be patient."

One day, I asked our commander, "Why are you killing mostly your own people, people from the North?"

He said, "We do not kill them because they are from the North, but because they are misbehaving."

I said, "Why do you kill those who try to escape?"

And he said, "Jesus did not ask his disciples to come with him, he just told them, 'Follow me.' But today Ugandans do not follow the Holy Spirit, so they must be forced."

I said, "People of northern Uganda would not refuse to follow you if what you did was truly right."

He said, "Stella, you are joking with the Holy Spirit. You don't know what we are doing. We are pretending we are bad, but we will be the first to enter God's Kingdom. One day you will believe in us and you will see we are God's people."

Many Ugandan government officials insist that Kony and his top commanders are motivated by greed and a thirst for personal power, rather than by any political or religious program. Indeed, it's impossible to assess the degree to which rebel actions are "truly" motivated by religion: the children we interviewed were all escapees from the rebels, non-believers more or less by definition. But it would be a mistake to dismiss out of hand the force of the rebels' beliefs: Kony's Lord's Resistance Army grew directly out of Alice Lakwena's Holy Spirit Movement, in which thousands of Acholi rebels met their deaths by walking into government bullets, armed with nothing more than stones, accepting Lakwena's assurance that the shea butter oil smeared on their chests would protect them.

Charles, fifteen:

> Kony was telling us that *Tipu Maleng* [the Holy Spirit] was
> protecting him. If a rebel who was a captive had ill feeling
> against Kony, Kony would be told by the spirits and would kill
> him. Spirits would also tell Kony who tried to escape.
>
> I don't know much about the Holy Spirit. Several times I was in
> Joseph Kony's hut, though, and I saw very many strange
> animals: you would find snakes, turtles, chameleons. I believe
> these are the instruments he used to communicate with the
> spirits.

George, fourteen:

> After we were first abducted, before they gave us food, they said
> we must become clean. We had to spread shea butter oil on our
> chests and our backs, because we were unclean, and had to
> become clean enough to eat with them.
>
> This is because we Acholi are a very bad people, and we must all
> become better before we can rule in our land. This is what the
> Holy Spirit has ordered. This also is why some people must be
> killed: we must become pure, and many Acholi do not follow the
> orders of the Holy Spirit anymore. Many of them are working
> with *jok* [spirits]. So they must be killed. This is what the rebels
> told me.

Lily, seventeen

> Everything they did was because of the *malaikas* (angels). For
> an example: there was a malaika from Sudan, that sent a
> message at one time that they should not sleep with their wives
> before fighting.
>
> And there were very many rules: before they crossed water they
> must pour water over their head. Also, you must not throw or
> step on certain stones. If a girl was during her period, she must
> not touch anything that a man will touch, and she must sit very

far away from the fire. Also, you must not greet anyone who is not a rebel with your hands.

Samuel, seventeen:

> Kony preached to us that no one should worry—he said the malaika said that no one should worry. He said the Holy Spirit knows the source of worry—the Holy Spirit says that if you worry or show signs of unhappiness, all your family members will be killed, or you will never be able to return to Uganda.

James, fourteen:

> The leader, Kony, would speak in tongues. Jok would speak through him—they would say that tomorrow such and such would happen. I only half-believed what he said. There were contradictions in what he said, so I didn't believe it all. But some of it was true. Like when Kony would order no eating—if you eat during the day you'll die in battle. I believed that, because I saw a boy who ate that day, and he later died in battle.

Stephen, seventeen:

> When you go to fight you make the sign of the cross first. If you fail to do this, you will be killed. You must also take oil and draw a cross on your chest, your forehead, and each shoulder, and you must make a cross in oil on your gun. They say that the oil is the power of the Holy Spirit. Some young children believe it—and those who have been there so long, five, seven, ten years, they believe in it very much.

> Also you take a small stone, you sew it on a cloth and wear it around your wrist like a watch. That is to prevent the bullet that might come, because in battle it is acting as a mountain. So those people on the other side will look at you, but they will see only a mountain, and the bullets will hit the mountain and not hurt you.

You also have water: they call it "clean water," and they pour it into a small bottle. If you go to the front, you also have a small stick, and you dip it in the bottle and fling the water out. This is a river and it drowns the bullet that might come to you.

Finally you wear a cross on a chain. But in the fighting you wrap it around your wrist and hold it in your hand. Should you make a mistake and not wear it on your hand, you will be killed.

Kony would say that he doesn't want *jogi* [spirits]. People working with jogi are witch-doctors, and if he got those people he would kill them.

But me, I was observing very carefully, and it is my observation that he was working with jogi himself. His spirit is not the real Holy Spirit, not Tipu Maleng. He is not working with God. Kony has control of where medicines were to be mixed, and when you see the materials, you know Kony is working with jok. I only saw from a distance. His jok is called Kivaro, and his jok is very powerful: when he said something is to be done, it is done according to his voice. When Kony talks he says it is Tipu Maleng talking, but it is Kivaro.

That is what I think. The Tipu Maleng could not work in this way to kill people.

Going into Battle

At some point, nearly all of the children end up in the midst of fighting. The rebels seem to rely mostly on teenage boys as fighters, but this is not a rigid rule; all children are expected to fight if necessary during raids on villages and stores. For planned battles, the rebels select boys to go and fight, but when ambushed by the Uganda People's Defense Force or the Sudan People's Liberation Army, all of the children are expected to take part in the fighting. Those who retreat are beaten.

The rebel commanders use the children as shields: when battle approaches, the children are sent to the front lines, while the commanders remain safely in the rear. At times, the children are told not to take cover, and they are beaten if they attempt to duck down or crouch behind trees or buildings. At other times, taking cover is permitted. There does not appear to be a pattern; it all depends on what orders the Holy Spirit gives Kony.

The children are told that those who obey the Holy Spirit will not be killed in battle: those who obey will be protected, while only those who have offended the Holy Spirit will die. Unknown numbers of captive children do die in the fighting, often killed by the bullets of government soldiers. Some of the children forced to the front are not even armed; caught in the crossfire, most of them die quickly.

Charles, fifteen:

> After training in Sudan, the rebels sent me back to Uganda. I was to be part of a group that would attack trading centers in Kitgum and abduct new children. I was well-armed, a soldier already. As we were returning, we were attacked by government soldiers. The frontline was somewhere ahead of where I was, and the commander said, "Run, run to the front-line!" It didn't matter whether you had a gun or not. If you did not run they would beat you with sticks. Many children without guns had to run to the front.

> You are not allowed to appear to be thinking too much. If you had a gun, you had to be firing all the time or you would be killed. And you were not allowed to take cover. The order from the Holy Spirit was not to take cover. You must have no fear, and stand up as you run into fire. This was because they said you would be protected by the Holy Spirit if you stood tall and had no fear. But if you took cover, the Holy Spirit would be angry and you would be shot dead by all the bullets.

> So many, so many were killed.

Samuel, seventeen:

> When the commanders sensed that there was an ambush ahead, they made us walk in a single line in front of them. The commanders were behind us directing us where to go. At the beginning you could hear gunshot sounds, and then, when you were right in the middle of the firing, you couldn't hear anything,

but only feel the bullets rushing by you, and pieces of them falling on you, and burning your skin.

The UPDF had very sophisticated weapons—when we met them, we often just took cover and ran.   The whole rebel group dispersed and ran.   We found each other later in the bush and began walking back to Uganda.   There were about twenty-five of us.   Our group had been eighty people, but I don't know what happened to the others in the fighting.   As we were walking, we met up with a rebel group near Palabek.   They put us under arrest for retreating, and took our weapons away—that was our punishment.

Thomas, fourteen:

At times when the war was coming some would be selected to go fight. You were just selected at random. It did not matter if you were young or old, or if you had a gun or not, you just had to go fight.

Going to the battle you must clap your hands and sing. There are many songs: some are prayer songs, some soldier songs. Some are both. For an example: "God, God, God, you come and help us, we have prepared to come to you." If you fail to clap your hands while you sing, a bullet will hit your hand. If you fail to sing, a bullet will hit your mouth. If you fail to walk always forward, a bullet will hit your leg.

We were told not to take cover. When you started fighting, as soon as you would fall down to take cover, the bullets would cut you up. If you stood strong you would be protected and there would be no need to retreat.

Stephen, seventeen:

It happens like this: Kony himself, he says he works with the Holy Spirit, and it talks to him, and he translates to the soldiers. So some days he says: "Today, you must burn the earth and kill the people." That is the reason the rebels make so much destruction.

When you have been selected to go and fight, you have been selected by the Holy Spirit. And so they say to you, you will go and fight with these people, but nobody will die, you will all come back after the battle. We have the Holy Spirit and it is going to work on you so that you will be protected, if you have been having good behavior. Maybe the bullet will hit your leg or your shoulder—but you will not die.

So many children were killed.

When they were killed in the battle, Kony would say, "Maybe they made an offense against the Holy Spirit." If you obeyed the Holy Spirit in all ways, you could not be killed. So if you died maybe it was because you did not follow his orders.

We used to question ourselves: this man, Kony, why is he sending us to go kill our brothers, our sisters, our fathers and mothers, to burn their houses, eat their food? Why are we having to do this? But there was no answer at all. We cannot see an answer to that question.

Escape

It is impossible to know the percentage of abducted children who die while in rebel captivity. The lucky children are those who manage to escape. Some escape shortly after capture, while others escape only after several years with the rebels.

Children who try unsuccessfully to escape from the camp or while on the march are killed, apparently without exception. But during battles, the rebels appear to relax their normally draconian rules: children who become separated from the group, but are later found, are treated as strays rather than as potential escapees, and receive only mild punishment.

As a result, many children wait until fighting breaks out to steal away in the confusion. Some simply drop their guns at an appropriate moment and surrender to government soldiers (UPDF) or to the Sudan People's Liberation Army (SPLA); the SPLA sends the children to Uganda People's Defense Force bases. Other children run away into the bush, and eventually approach a civilian to request assistance. Civilians usually bring escaped children to the Uganda People's Defense Force, although it is possible that some escaping children are killed by civilians who, viewing the children as rebels, shoot first and ask questions later. Several children spoke of near-escapes from civilians who wanted to kill them.

We heard scattered reports of captured children being charged with treason, although government spokespersons denied that this ever occurs. By all accounts, the Uganda People's Defense Force and Sudan People's Liberation Army treat child rebels who surrender or escape with sympathy, and release them to trauma counseling centers or their families after interrogation.

While fear and bewilderment had left many of the children we interviewed with only the blurriest memories of their experiences with the rebels, most children became animated and detailed in their descriptions of their escapes. For these children, perhaps, escape was a literal return to real life.

Lily, seventeen:

> We were by the river between Gulu and Kitgum when we entered a UPDF ambush. People began to run and there were bombs everywhere. I ran into the deep water to hide from the bombs. I had a bag on my back that I was carrying, and it got wet and heavy and pulled me down until the water covered me. I dropped it and began to float in the river. Finally I reached a certain place where my legs touched a stone, and I stood there. The fighting was still going on, and bodies were falling into the water beside me. I saw some tall grasses in the shallow water, and I went and hid inside the tall grass. A UPDF airplane came, and I feared it would bomb me, so I stayed hidden until it left. Then there was no more noise of bullets and I got up.

> I heard someone crying. It was a little girl who was drowning in the river, and she was crying, "Come and help me, the water is taking me and I am dying!" I could not reach her because the water was too fast and deep. There was an old man and a young boy of eight or nine, and the little girl called to the old man for help, but his legs were swollen and he could not walk. We had to leave her.

> The old man said to me, "My daughter, pick for me that stick for me to lean on, and let us walk to Gulu town." So we began to

walk with the young boy, who held a small jerrycan full of ground nuts. Then we heard voices, and UPDF people appeared, and began shooting at us. The young boy threw away the jerrycan and we began to run.

In the confusion I became separated from the old man and the young boy, and for a long time I was lost in the bush. I could not find any homes or anything to eat. I moved, and I could not find anyone. I thought, "I cannot move anymore." In the night I heard wild animals pass me. Once I came across a place where people had been cooking, and I thought I was saved, but when I looked closely I saw it was a fire that had been made by the rebels. You can tell because the rebels don't use stones for setting fires, because the malaikas say they must not: if stones are used in fires, they say they will burst like bombs upon you. Also, the malaikas forbid cigarettes, while at UPDF fires you see cigarette butts.

After many days I came across a village and saw two women. They were washing their hands to eat. I asked them, "What is the name of this place?" They told me to enter inside their home, and they told me to wash my hands and eat. They asked me many questions, and people from all through the village came to see me, then they took me to bathe and put me to bed. In the morning they said, "You cannot stay here, because the UPDF will harm us if we keep a rebel girl here. " So they took me to barracks, where I stayed for some weeks, and then they brought me back to my family in Gulu.

Teddy, thirteen:

As we were walking, we came to a thick forest of bamboo. I had been given old gumboots to wear, and they had become filled up with water, so I stopped to empty my boots and the rebels went on ahead. As I was emptying my boots, I heard a sudden noise of bullets being fired. I looked around and could see no rebels. There were bullets all around, flying past me. I began to run, and although a bullet hit me in the leg, I kept running. I ran until I came to a village. When people saw me, they screamed and ran away, so I shouted, "People, help me! I am a civilian like yourselves, I am only escaping from the rebels. Please take me to a leader here."

I had forgotten that I was still holding a gun. That is why people were running from me. Someone said, "If you are truly escaping, then throw down your gun!" So I did, and they led me to the home of the village leader.

All of my leg was swollen and I could not walk well now, but the wife of the leader was very kind and started nursing me. I spent the night at the home of the leader, and the next day he took me to a government detachment.

Catherine, seventeen:

There was to be a big fight that day. The Arabs and Kony's group and another group of rebels commanded by Juma Oris [leader of the West Nile Bank Front] had come together and were fighting the Sudan People's Liberation Army. They had ordered all the pregnant women to be taken in a lorry to Juba. We could hear the bombs from afar.

A woman ordered me to go get water, so we girls went to the well. We heard gunfire very close by and ran into the bush. I couldn't run well because I had hurt my foot when we were digging. I didn't know what to do and tried to go back to the camp. I hid in a trench.

I could hear tanks entering the camp. It was getting dark. Bullets are red at night. I was praying. I got up slowly when things became quiet. There were dead bodies all around in the camp. No one was left in the camp. The rebels had all run away or were dead. I heard people speaking Kiswahili, and I knew they must be the Sudan People's Liberation Army, because the Arabs and Kony's rebels don't speak Swahili. One of the SPLA found me and started yelling. Another SPLA said that if I was a girl, I might be one of the Aboke girls. I felt so happy when I heard this.   They took me to the Uganda government soldiers, who were in Sudan, and then I was flown to Gulu.

Ellen, fourteen:

> My escape happened in the fighting against the Sudan People's Liberation Army. We were sent to fetch water, and we said to each other, "Let us each run our own way." So we started running.
>
> After a time nine of us found each other again, and we walked until we came to a certain home among the Dinkas. The villagers surrounded us and said we were rebels, and we should be lined up and killed. But an elder from that place came, and said, "You do not kill these young children!" So instead they asked us if we had eaten, and they made some porridge for us, then took us to the Sudan People's Liberation Army, and the Sudan People's Liberation Army put us in a vehicle and brought us back to Uganda.

The Future

Children who escape from rebel captivity are in poor shape: they are usually in lice-ridden rags, covered with sores, scarred from beatings and bullet wounds. According to World Vision's Robby Muhumuza, the children arrive at trauma counseling centers "sick, malnourished, with low appetite. They have guilt feelings, are depressed and with low self-esteem . . . . They have swollen feet, rough skin, chest infections . . . they tend to be aloof . . . with little confidence in themselves or others. They tend to lapse into absentmindedness as well as swift mood changes."[12]

Many of the children—especially the girls, who are routinely given to rebel leaders as "wives"—also have sexually transmitted diseases: "They arrive with gonorrhea, syphilis or sores, skin rash and complaints of abdominal pain and backache."[13] At World Vision in Gulu, 70 to 80 percent of the children newly

---

[12] Robby Muhumuza, *The Gun Children of Gulu* (Uganda: World Vision, December 1995), pp. 9-10.

[13] Ibid.

arriving at the center test positive for at least one sexually transmitted disease.[14] Some of the girls are pregnant, while others, who tested negative for pregnancy, have stopped having their menstrual periods because of malnutrition and stress.[15] The trauma counseling centers do not test the children for HIV, reasoning that after their experiences in the bush, the children are not yet psychologically ready to be told that they may have contracted a fatal illness. But with HIV infection rates of 25 percent in parts of Gulu and Kitgum, it is overwhelmingly likely that many of the children—especially the girls—have become infected.

Counselors and children's advocates criticize the Uganda People's Defense Force for not providing escaped children with adequate medical care while the children are in UPDF control. "They don't always give them treatment right away," says Richard Oneka, a counselor. "Sometimes by the time they reach us, they've been with the UPDF for weeks without seeing a doctor."[16]

The Uganda People's Defense Force also sometimes brings recently escaped children to appear at public rallies, to drum up popular support for the fight against the rebels. This practice, too, is sharply criticized by children's advocates: "They display the children, and read out their names, which only increases the likelihood of rebel reprisals against the child or his family," explains Paulinus Nyeko of Gulu Human Rights Focus. "Also, they give details on how the child escaped. The rebels come to hear of it, and that makes it hard for other children to escape. The army is just using the children."[17]

In its 1996 report to the U.N.Committee on the Rights of the Child, the Ugandan government affirmed its general commitment "to improve the lives of . . . child soldiers" and its "special concern" for children abducted by rebels.[18]

---

[14] Human Rights Watch interview, World Vision's Gulu Tramatized Children of War Project, Gulu, May 30, 1997.

[15] Human Rights Watch interview, Concerned Parents of Aboke, Lira, May 27, 1997.

[16] Human Rights Watch interview, Richard Oneko, Counselor, Gulu Save the Children Organization, Gulu, May 30, 1997.

[17] Human Rights Watch interview, Gulu, May 30, 1997.

[18] Government of Uganda, report on the implementation of the U.N.Convention on the Rights of the Child, 1 February 1996. The Ugandan Constitution lays out certain basic rights of children: "Every child has a right to know and be cared for by his parents . . . . a child has a right to a basic education . . . . No child shall be deprived of medical care,

Nonetheless, the Uganda Child Rights NGO Network (UCRNN) has been critical of the government's response to the crisis in the north, noting that while the Museveni government provided "special services" for children who were caught up in civil wars of the early 1980s (when Museveni's guerrilla army fought the Obote and Okello regimes), "children caught up in the armed rebellion in northern Uganda since 1987 have not received adequate support from the government." According to UCRNN, "no government programmes or resources have been identified" for children abducted by the Lord's Resistance Army. UCRNN has called upon the government to "take concrete measures to address the needs of children caught up in armed conflict" and to "establish adequate responses for the long-term support of these children." [19]

---

education or any other social and economic benefit." Constitution of the Republic of Uganda, enacted September 22, 1995, promulgated October 8, 1995. Chapter Four, Paragraph 17. The Government's duties with regard to children are elaborated in the Children Statute of 1996, which entered into force in August 1997. The statute defines a child as "a person below the age of eighteen years," (Part II, paragraph 3), and states that "whenever the state, a court, a local authority or any person determines any question with respect [to] the upbringing of a child . . . the child's welfare shall be the paramount consideration." (First Schedule, paragraph 1). Specifically, "A child shall have the right . . . . to a just call on any social amenities or other resources available in any situation of armed conflict or natural or man-made disasters." (First Schedule, Paragraph 4b).

The constitution also declares that Ugandan children have "all the rights set out in the U.N. Convention on the rights of the child and the OAU Charter on the rights and welfare of the child. . . ." (First Schedule, paragraph 4c). The U.N. Convention on the Rights of the Child states that "States parties shall take all feasible measures to ensure that persons who have not attained the age of fifteen years do not a direct part in hostilities . . . . In accordance with their obligations under international humanitarian law to protect the civilian population in armed conflicts, States Parties shall take all feasible measures to ensure protection and care of children who are affected by an armed conflict." Convention on the Rights of the Child, Article 38. The African Charter on the Rights and Welfare of the Child reiterates these principles in Article 22: "States parties to the present charter shall, in accordance with their obligations under international humanitarian law, protect the civilian population in armed conflicts and shall take all feasible measures to ensure the protection and care of children who are affected by armed conflicts. Such rules shall also apply to children in situations of internal armed conflicts, tension and strife."

[19] Uganda Child Rights NGO Network, "Response to the Government of Uganda Country Report on the Implementation of the U.N. Convention on the Rights of the Child," pp. iii, 12.

Some of the children who escape from the rebels go immediately home to their villages, and some return to their boarding schools, but many end up staying, for a time, at the trauma centers operated by World Vision or the Gulu Save the Children Organization (GUSCO). Conditions in the centers are poor: too many children in small huts and tents, too few trained counselors, and not enough for the children to do. At one center, children are taught basic skills like carpentry, tailoring and bicycle repair, but at the others, the children spend much of their time just sitting around, playing card games or staring into space.

But at least the centers feel safe to the children: at the centers, they are surrounded by other children who have gone through similar experiences, and cared for by supportive, non-judgmental adults. This is not always the case outside of the centers: according to Robby Muhumuza, children who return home sometimes find that other families with young relatives still in captivity are "jealous of those who have returned." Some people also blame the children for rebel atrocities. Those villagers who had themselves suffered at the hands of Lord's Resistance Army rebels are sometimes "antagonistic, labeling the children 'rebels.'"[20] Occasionally, children face physical threats from community members who identify them as perpetrators of atrocities.[21]

For girls, in a culture which regards non-marital sex as "defilement," the difficulties are even greater: reviled for being "rebels," the girls may also find themselves ostracized for having been "wives." They fear "shame, humiliation and rejection by their relatives and possible future husbands." They may suffer "continual taunts from boys and men [who say they are] used products that have lost their taste."[22]

For many children, lack of community acceptance is the least of their troubles. "Many of these children have parents who were killed during their abductions," explains World Vision's Charles Wotman. "Others have families, but they have been displaced, and no one knows where they are."[23] Children without families worry that they will be unable to support themselves. Even those children

---

[20] Muhumuza, "Gun Children," p. 11.

[21] Human Rights Watch interview, Lacor Hospital, Gulu, May 29, 1997.

[22] Robby Muhumuza, *Girls Under Guns* (Uganda: World Vision, December, 1995), pp. 12-13.

[23] Human Rights Watch interview, Kiryandongo, May 26, 1997.

with supportive homes and communities fear leaving the centers, because of the danger of being re-abducted and killed.

Sharon, thirteen:

> I haven't been home since I was abducted, and I don't know where my family is. I met my cousin in Gulu and she told me that after I escaped, my uncle was killed. She said my mother and family ran away.
>
> I want to finish my course in tailoring here, and try to look for a place to stay in Gulu town. I won't go home—I think I would be abducted again, and maybe killed.

Patricia, fifteen:

> I'm afraid to go home because I'll be abducted again and killed. Home is not safe. My parents came to see me when I was in Gulu. They were so happy to see me. They said they thought I was dead. But they told me to stay away, to stay at [the trauma counseling center], because home is not safe.

Samuel, seventeen:

> I've been here at the center for three weeks now. My mother came to see me last week. She told me that my other two brothers [who were abducted with me] have not returned. I hope they are still alive. I do not want to think about them.
>
> My mother said that shortly after me and my brothers were abducted, the Lord's Resistance Army attacked our home again, and looted, and burned it down. My mother has moved to Atiak trading center. She says home is not yet secure, and that she will look for a home for me in Gulu town. I want to take vocational training here at the center.
>
> I think the world should think about Kony's actions because he is abusing children so much. Children also want to enjoy peace like their fathers and mothers enjoyed when they were young.

In the short term, the children face many direct threats to their lives and livelihoods. But the long-term psychological effects of their experiences can only be guessed at. For many children, fears about the future are accompanied by memories of the past, memories of their own pain and of the atrocities they witnessed and took part in:

William, ten:

> I am afraid to go back home to my village, because the rebels are still there in plenty. I fear they will kill me if they come to know of me here. I was in primary three when I was abducted, and I would like to go back to school, if there is somewhere that is safe. I don't know. I am sad now. The other thing I would like to say is that I experienced the deaths of many children. I wish there could be a solution.

Thomas, fourteen:

> When I think back, the hardest thing was seeing other children being killed. That was the hardest thing. The second hardest thing was the brutal life—someone can be beaten on no grounds at all. I don't know what I will do, now: I would like to go back home but it is still unsafe, and I fear the rebels coming again. I am learning bicycle repair here, but when I must leave I fear having no tools. I do not know how I will support myself.

Molly, seventeen:

> I have been back at school now for almost three months. I tend to forget, almost, that it ever happened to me. But it often comes to me suddenly. I look around in class and see the seats that are still empty because of our girls who are still in the bush, and I think that the bad things that for me are over are still happening to them, and then I feel sad and afraid.

Teddy, thirteen:

> A thing I remember is how if you tried to escape, they would put you in the center of the circle and stab at you with bayonets or

pangas. Sometimes little pieces of the bodies would come off. This is what I remember most often.

As for me now, I am very happy here for the time right now. I would like to go home and continue a normal education, but there is nobody to support me. There is nobody to care for me. I pray to God to help.

For other children, it isn't the waking memories that are worst, but the dreams. "These children don't want to remember what they've been through," says James Kazini, commander of the army's Fourth Division in Gulu. "My wife and I had several of the escaped girls staying in our house, before they went back to school, and they were all dreaming in the night: at one time, one of the girls woke us shouting, because she said she was seeing blood everywhere, blood floating out of the bed." [24]

Stephen, seventeen:

I went to the elders and I was cleansed: I had to be cleansed because I killed. It does not matter that you did not wish to kill. You still have killed and must become clean again. For me, I am older, and I think I will be all right. But I am thinking that it is the young boys and young girls who will not be all right.

I am very much interested to go back to school. So for now I am just here, and I am feeling okay. But I don't feel yet free, because of some dreams that can come at night, because of the bad things that happened to me in the bush. Killing people, dead bodies, the sound of gunshots—sometimes you wake up and it is as though that is what is still taking place. Life with the rebels was really very bad.

Timothy, fourteen

I don't know what I will do in the future. Since I've been here [at the trauma counseling center], I haven't seen my family, and am sad that they haven't come. I don't know anything about

---

[24] Human Rights Watch interview, Gulu, May 30, 1997.

them—I have no news. I can't go home. I'll be re-abducted
and killed straightaway. At least here, I feel safer than at home.
 I dream at night of being re-abducted, or that I am still a
captive, walking somewhere.

Susan, sixteen:

I feel so bad about the things that I did. It disturbs me so much,
that I inflicted death on other people. When I go home I must
do some traditional rites because I have killed. I must perform
these rites and cleanse myself. I still dream about the boy from
my village who I killed. I see him in my dreams and he is
talking to me and saying I killed him for nothing, and I am
crying.

Relevant International Humanitarian Standards

The human rights abuses of the Lord's Resistance Army shock the
conscience, and violate the most elementary principles of international
humanitarian law. The LRA's abuses of children's rights are both too numerous
and too self-evident to make an exhaustive list of relevant international human
rights standards necessary. Most pertinently, however, the LRA's actions violate
the provisions of Common Article 3 of the Geneva Conventions of 1949, which
lays out the minimum humanitarian rules applicable to internal armed conflicts:

In the case of armed conflict not of an international character
occurring in the territory of one of the High Contracting Parties,
each Party to the conflict shall be bound to apply, as a minimum,
the following provisions:

(1) Persons taking no active part in the hostilities, including
members of armed forces who have laid down their arms and
those placed *hors de combat* by sickness, wounds, detention, or
any other cause, shall in all circumstances be treated humanely,
without any adverse distinction founded on race, colour, religion
or faith, sex, birth or wealth, or any other similar criteria.

To this end the following acts are and shall remain prohibited at any time and in any place whatsoever with respect to the above-mentioned persons:

(a) violence to life and person, in particular murder of all kinds, or mutilation, cruel treatment and torture;

(b) taking of hostages;

(c) outrages upon personal dignity, in particular humiliating and degrading treatment;

(d) the passing of sentences and the carrying out of executions without previous judgment pronounced by a regularly constituted court, affording all the judicial guarantees which are recognized as indispensable by civilized peoples.

(2) The wounded and sick shall be collected and cared for.[25]

Since Common Article 3 of the Geneva Conventions is binding on "each Party to the conflict"—that is, it is binding on both governmental and non-governmental forces—the Lord's Resistance Army currently stands in flagrant violation of international humanitarian law.

---

[25] The protections established by Common Article 3 are developed and supplemented by Protocol II to the Geneva Conventions of 1949, which applies to internal armed conflicts "which take place in the territory of a High Contracting Party between its armed forces and dissident armed forces or other organized armed groups which, under responsible command, exercise such contol over a part of its territory as to enable them to carry out sustained and concerted military operations and to implement this Protocol." (Article 1, 1). Protocol II reiterates the fundamental guarantees laid out in Common Article 3, and adds a range of additional requirements for armed groups to whom the protocol applies. In circumstances in which Protocol II does not directly apply, it is generally seen as providing interpretive guidance on the implementation of Common Article 3, which establishes only minimum humanitarian standards. Of particular relevance here are several of the Protocol II provisions which relate specifically to children: for instance, Article 4(3)(c) states that "children who have not attained the age of fifteen years shall neither be recruited in the armed forces or groups nor allowed to take part in hostilities." Article 4(3)(d) states that "the special protection provided in this Article to children who have not attained the age of fifteen years shall remain applicable to them if they take a direct part in hostilities despite the provisions of subparagraph (c) and are captured." Protocol II was ratified by Uganda in 1991.

Currently, the Geneva Conventions and the U.N. Convention on the Rights of the Child establish fifteen as the minimum age at which states that have ratified these treaties may recruit children into their armed forces. Since the Lord's Resistance Army is a nongovernmental force, it is not a party to these treaties (although it remains bound by Common Article 3 of the Geneva Conventions, cited above). Nonetheless, these treaties establish clear principles of customary international law with regard to the use of children as combatants. Serious violations of the rules and customs of war, including the forced recruitment of children into armed groups, should be punished by law.

The 1996 United Nations Study on the Impact of Armed Conflict on Children documented the tragedy of child soldiers throughout the world; as Graca Machel, who headed the study, says, "War violates every right of the child—the right to life, the right to grow up in a family environment, the right to health, the right to survival and full development and the right to be nurtured and protected, among others."[26] In the study, Graca Machel also recommended that the minimum age for recruitment and participation in armed forces be raised from fifteen to eighteen.

It is Human Rights Watch's position that no one under the age of eighteen should be recruited (either voluntarily or involuntarily) into any armed forces, whether governmental or nongovernmental in nature.[27]

---

[26] Graca Machel, Statement to the Third Committee of the U.N.General Assembly, November 8, 1996.

[27] Human Rights Watch supports current efforts to raise to eighteen the age at which people can take part in armed conflicts. This effort is being spearheaded by the United Nations Working Group on a Draft Optional Protocol to the Convention on the Rights of the Child on the Involvement of Children in Armed Conflict. (The Draft Optional Protocol is included in the appendix to this report). For other Human Rights Watch reports dealing with child soldiers in various parts of the world, see, for instance, Human Rights Watch/Asia, "Burma: Children's Rights and the Rule of Law," *A Human Rights Watch Short Report*, vol.9, no.1(c), January 1997; Human Rights Watch/Africa & Human Rights Watch Children's Rights Project, *Children of Sudan: Slaves, Street Children and Child Soldiers* (New York: Human Rights Watch, 1995), and Human Rights Watch/ Africa & Human Rights Watch Children's Rights Project, *Easy Prey: Child Soldiers in Liberia* (New York: Human Rights Watch, 1994).

III. OTHER EFFECTS OF THE CONFLICT IN THE NORTH

Piny dong oloyo acholi woko pi lweny man.
("The Acholi are helpless because of the insecurity in the north.")
> -Title of a song written by children at the World Vision Center at Kiryandongo

Who will protect us? Even in Amin's time, we were not killed like this.
> - Hon. Livingstone Okello-Okello, MP for Kitgum[28]

Abducted children are not the only victims of the conflict in the north. The conflict, which has now persisted for over a decade, has taken the lives of thousands of civilians of all ages. Some have been killed by the rebels during raids; others have been caught in the crossfire between rebels and government soldiers. While at times several weeks go by with few rebel attacks, during other periods, the death toll is astounding: during a single two-week period in July 1996, for instance, violence took the lives of forty soldiers, thirty-two rebels and 225 civilians. Between January 6 and January 10, 1997, 400 civilians were slaughtered during a rebel attack in Kitgum.[29]

Northern Uganda today faces an acute humanitarian crisis. The two northern districts of Gulu and Kitgum, the homeland of the Acholi people, have been hardest hit: relief agencies estimate that over 240,000 people are currently displaced from their homes and villages,[30] while some local officials estimate that

---

[28] Human Rights Watch interview, Kampala, June 2, 1997.

[29] The Parliament of Uganda, "Report of the Committee on Defense and Internal Affairs on the War in Northern Uganda," Minority Report by Hon. Norbert Mao and Hon. Daniel Omara Atubo, January 1997.

[30] UNICEF Background Situation Report, June 1997.

the figure is as high as two million displaced people.[31] In Kitgum, nearly half of the displaced people are children, and more than a third of those children have been orphaned by the war.[32]

The infrastructure in Gulu and Kitgum is in a state of collapse. The constant danger of land mines and rebel ambushes has made many of the region's few roads unsafe for travel. Rebel attacks destroyed thousands of homes. Agriculture has come to a standstill in parts of the region, since the insecurity has forced people to flee their homes and abandon their fields.

Education, too, has stopped in many places. The rebels target schools and teachers, and in the last year, in Gulu alone, more than seventy-five schools have been burnt down by the rebels, and 215 teachers have been killed. Many more teachers have been abducted or have fled the region. An estimated 60,000 school-aged children have been displaced, and during 1996, the number of functioning schools in Gulu fell from 199 to sixty-four.[33]

Attacks on schools are an efficient way for the rebels to abduct many children at once. In October 1996, for instance, the rebels raided St. Mary's, a Catholic girls' boarding school in the town of Aboke, in Apac district. The rebels arrived in the middle of the night, and entered the school through a window. They destroyed a of school vehicle, ransacked the school clinic, attempted to burn down a number of school buildings, and abducted 139 girls, aged mostly fifteen to seventeen.[34] The scale of the Aboke abductions was unusual, as was the rebel

---

[31] Gulu District Emergency Plan, May-June 1997. Since the total population of Gulu and Kitgum combined is roughly 700,000, UNICEF's figure seems more plausible. (*Uganda Districts Information Handbook*, 1995/96 Edition (Kampala: Fountain Publishers, Inc., 1995)).

[32] UNICEF Background Situation Report, June 1997.

[33] Gulu District Emergency Plan.

[34] One hundred and nine of the Aboke girls were released shortly after the raid, when Sister Rachele Fassera, the deputy headmistress of the school, succeeded in following the rebels into the bush. She confronted the rebels and begged them to release the children, urging them to take her in the girls stead. Faced with her pleas, the rebels permitted her to leave with 109 of the girls, keeping only thirty as captives. Sister Rachele's courageous actions helped bring public attention to the Lord's Resistance Army's practice of abducting children, and the subsequent efforts of Sister Rachele Fassera and the Concerned Parents of Aboke have forced the Museveni government to begin negotiations with Sudan in an effort to obtain the release of the remaining Aboke captives. Of the thirty girls kept by the rebels

incursion into Apac, but the rebel tactic of raiding schools is typical, and has gravely disrupted the north's educational system.

The health care system in the north, always rudimentary, has almost collapsed. Many of those who are wounded in the fighting receive little or no medical attention; as a result, figures giving the number of dead and wounded are almost certainly too low, since many deaths and injuries never come to the attention of the authorities. Rebel raids on clinics and dispensaries have diminished the store of medicines available, and the instability has caused many health workers to flee. This has disrupted most basic non-emergency services, including immunization campaigns. Officially, there are thirty rural health units in Gulu, but as of May 1997, only fourteen remained in operation.[35]

The results are predictable: by almost any health care indicator, Gulu and Kitgum lag far behind other parts of Uganda. At the end of 1995, for instance, the infant mortality rate in Gulu was 172 per thousand live births, compared to eighty per thousand live births in Kampala. Most estimates suggest that the HIV infection rate in the region hovers at around 25 percent of the population.[36] And AIDS deaths compound all of the region's other problems, further straining health care resources, rendering immune-compromised people more vulnerable to other diseases, and leaving still more children orphaned.

The health crisis has been greatly exacerbated by the government policy of encouraging civilians to leave rural areas and move to "protected camps" near Uganda People's Defense Force military installations. The rationale behind the protected camps is straightforward: by concentrating the civilian population in a few well-defined areas, the army hopes both to simplify the task of protecting people from rebel attacks and make it harder for the rebels to find food by raiding villages. But in practice, the protected camps have been, at best, a mixed blessing for the internally displaced people of Gulu and Kitgum: tens of thousands of them thronged to the camps, only to find that virtually no provision had been made for sanitation or sustenance.

---

after Sister Rachele's intervention, nine had escaped as of May 1997. We interviewed six of the nine escapees during our visit to St. Mary's on May 28, 1997, and we collected written testimonials from over a hundred of the other girls. A number of the most representative testimonials are reproduced in the appendix to this report.

[35] Gulu District Emergency Plan.

[36] This estimate was given to us by a number of different journalists, lawyers and doctors.

In the protected camp at Pabbo, in Gulu district, for instance, a displaced population of over 30,000 relies for water on only two boreholes, one of which was not functional as of May. The likelihood of any improvement in the situation is minimal, because the district lacks the staff and equipment to fix breakdowns: according to the Gulu Disaster Management Committee, "most of the [district's] field crew were laid off in the recent restructuring exercise [and] all the vehicles attached to the water dept. in this district are broken down except one which is moving but in very bad mechanical condition." Along with the paltry water supply in Pabbo, no latrines had been created for the camp. And Pabbo is not unusual; according to the Gulu Disaster Management Committee, "[T]he whole situation is pathetic . . . . Suffering in long queues, and swamps of flies over the stinking garbage and human excreta is the order of the day in most camps."[37]

Unsurprisingly, limited water, poor sanitary facilities and minimal provision of medical care in the protected camps has led to thousands of deaths each month.[38] Ten of the twenty-four camps in Gulu district are situated in areas with no health care facilities at all, and a recent survey in three of the camps found that 41.9 percent of the children were malnourished. Epidemics of measles, malaria and dysentery kill off many of the weakest in the camps In Pabbo alone, there were more than four thousand deaths during the month of February 1997 (more recent figures are not available).[39]

A local doctor's words give some sense of the scope of the humanitarian crisis in the north:

---

[37] Gulu District Emergency Plan.

[38] "11 Years on, War Wracked Acholi only getting Worse," *The Monitor* (Kampala), May 25, 1997. Despite the extremely dangerous conditions in the protected camps, a number of people interviewed by Human Rights Watch charged that government soldiers often force unwilling civilians into the camps, warning them that if they remain in rural areas, the Uganda People's Defense Force will consider them to be rebel collaborators and may kill them. A number of our interviewees also complained that government soldiers do not provide the camps with adequate military protection, and do not respond quickly enough to reports of rebel activity. Since Human Rights Watch's mission to Uganda was primarily concerned with the abduction of children, we were unable to investigate these allegations or assess their validity.

[39] There were 1457 deaths from malaria, 14 from measles, 1558 from diarrhea, 490 from "diarrhea with blood," sixteen from malnutrition and 480 from upper respiratory tract disorder like pneumonia. Gulu District Office Morbidity Data for Protected Camps, February 1997.

In 1995, we saw a total of 335 war injuries at this hospital. In 1996, we saw 117 victims of land mines, and 515 gunshot wounds. This year, from January through late April, we saw fourteen mine victims and 155 other war wound victims. Remember those are just the people who we see—most people never come to the hospital.

The majority of children come to us because of the indirect effects of the war. When there is inadequate food, children are usually the first to become ill. We see epidemics, malnutrition, malaria, and most of the outbreaks start in the protected camps. More children are sick, and those who are sick are sicker than usual. Now the malnutrition wards are full of children from the camps. In the camps, children are very sick; many of them are dying. Most of them never get to the hospital.

The government thought that protected camps would deny the rebels access to support and information, but it was done in such a hurry, and without planning, that really it was a source of great suffering to the people. Last year, when people began surging to the towns, the population in Gulu town swelled by 70,000 people, and a measles epidemic struck. About 20 percent of the children brought into the hospital died. In the villages, maybe half of the children who got sick died, because they got no medical care.

If there had been prior planning, if there had been planning for sanitation, food, water, and medicines . . . . but by herding people into the camps, just like that, this cost a lot of lives. Some of the camps have only a few soldiers nearby, and people say, "They are using us as human shields." So if the rebels try to attack the soldiers, it is civilians who are killed. And if the people leave the camp, if they even just go home for a day to try to find food, then they are targeted by the rebels for having gone to the camps. Many people lose their lives that way.

The problem is that we don't see an end to the problem. When you have a problem and you think it's coming to an end, then you say, let's persevere. But I really don't see how this is going to end. I foresee unlimited suffering ... the last two years have been the worst in ten years. We cannot do anything, we cannot go outside in the community, we cannot do our work. We are trapped, we can't move on the roads. So now the sense of hopelessness is the biggest problem with the people. And this is the easiest situation for the rebels to operate in. The people have no will except to surrender.

It has to stop, it must stop. It is painful to live in a place where the rebels are around, and you have to hide your own children in the bush and bring food to them, to try to keep them safe. The rebels' main interest is in the children, it's how they recruit. Children are malleable, they can be easily managed. The rebels don't care if some die: they just abduct more. And there is really no protection for these children. If they were taking adults, I would not care as much, I would perhaps say that this kind of thing is just part of the problem with us here in Uganda—but these children are just used. They are not the ones who voted for Museveni. If our country is troubled the fault is not theirs.

When you are in the medical field, you are trained always to look for solutions. But I cannot see one here. [40]

According to Paulinus Nyeko of Gulu Human Rights Focus, civilians frequently complain of harassment and human rights abuses by the Ugandan People's Defense Force, including robbery, rape and torture.[41] Since the focus of our investigation was on the abduction of children, we were not able to look into these charges, but we asked military officials if they were aware of them. Lieutenant Bantirinza Shaban, the public relations officer for the UPDF in Gulu, confirmed that he was aware of such allegations, and attributed any such incidents to "communication problems" stemming from "ethnic difficulties and language differences."[42]

---

[40] Human Rights Watch interview, Gulu, May 29, 1997.

[41] Human Rights Watch interview, Gulu, May 30, 1997. These allegations were repeated to us by numerous other NGO representatives.

[42] Human Rights Watch interview, Gulu, May 29, 1997.

Colonel James Kazini, commander of the UPDF Fourth Division, had a different explanation: he attributed such abuses to the Acholi soldiers, saying, "If anything, it is local Acholi soldiers causing the problems. It's the cultural background of the people here: they are very violent. It's genetic." He expressed his regret that Ugandan law prohibits summary justice against soldiers found to have committed abuses: "We used to have field court martials, and try and sentence them right in the market place. We used to just kill them. But now the president does not allow it . . . soldiers accused of misbehaving are taken to the police and charged."[43]

---

[43] Human Rights Watch interview, Gulu, May 30, 1997.

IV. THE HISTORY AND CAUSES OF THE CONFLICT

To think about it, you feel a headache.
                        - Sister Bruna Barollo, Camboni Sisters [44]

But where is the world? Why do they not like the Acholi? What
have we done that the world should just watch us suffer?
                        - Andres Banya, Acholi Development Association [45]

During our stay in Uganda, we were struck repeatedly by the contrast between north and south. The international press has been full of glowing reports on the prosperity and stability Uganda has enjoyed under President Museveni, and the atmosphere in Kampala appears to bear this out: the streets are bustling, there is construction everywhere, and Kampala enjoys a reputation as one of Africa's safest cities.

From the air, the south is a blanket of green farms, plantations and forests, with small houses dotting the landscape. Flying north, the scene gradually changes. Houses become mixed with huts, and ultimately give way to huts entirely. In Gulu, the observer sees a landscape filled with burnt huts, deserted compounds, and abandoned fields. There is virtually no traffic on the few roads.

It's only a four-hour drive from Kampala to Gulu or Kitgum, but it might as well be a thousand miles. Cultural and linguistic differences ensure that residents of southern Uganda have few social reasons to venture north, and the relative under-development of the far north makes it unlikely that southerners will visit Gulu or Kitgum for commercial reasons. The danger of mines and ambushes along northern roads further diminishes southerners' incentive to visit their Acholi compatriots, and the lack of telecommunications infrastructure in the north makes even phone contact rare.

As journalist Cathy Watson observes, "There's no Acholi elite in the south, and so there's no one to put the north on the agenda or keep it in people's minds. The north just slides off the map."[46] These factors, in combination, mean that southern Ugandans often have little awareness of the atrocities and the humanitarian crisis in the north.

---

[44] Human Rights Watch interview, Kampala, May 20, 1997.

[45] Human Rights Watch interview, Kampala, June 3, 1997.

[46] Human Rights Watch interview, Kampala, May 26, 1997.

The apparent senselessness of the conflict in the north exacerbates the problem. Although they are ostensibly dedicated to the military overthrow of the Museveni government, the rebels of the Lord's Resistance Army instead seem to concentrate on attacking the civilian population. Indeed, the rebels prey largely upon the Acholi people, the very ethnic group to which most of them belong. To many southerners, then, the conflict is not only distant but incomprehensible: it is Acholi slaughtering Acholi, for no discernible reason.

To the people of the north, however, and especially to the Acholi, the rebels are much more than a distant and incomprehensible nuisance. With hundreds and sometimes thousands dying each month, with more children abducted every day, with crops destroyed, homes looted and burnt, and epidemic diseases prevelent in the through the protected camps, the conflict has devastated the region in an unprecedented way.

This lends a certain urgency to the problem of understanding the roots and sources of the conflict. Bewilderment about the conflict is understandable: during our investigation we heard many tentative theories about why the conflict continues, but few people were willing to hazard a definitive explanation, and the rebels themselves are a black box. We heard stories and counter-stories, some more persuasive than others, but none ultimately satisfying. This, however, does not mean that there is no reason for the violence; it instead suggests that the reasons are many and deep, and fully disentangling them may not be possible in the end.

To the limited extent that the conflict has received foreign press coverage, the media has tended to present the Lord's Resistance Army in straightforward, if disapproving, terms: to the media, the Lord's Resistance Army is a group of militant Christian fundamentalists who seek to restore a government based upon the Ten Commandments. *The New York Times* calls them "blood-thirsty . . . self-styled revolutionaries and Christian fundamentalist rebels."[47] CNN calls them "a Christian cult . . . led by a former Catholic named Kony."[48] *The Guardian* calls Kony a "Christian fanatic."[49]

---

[47] "Christian Rebels Wage a War of Terror in Uganda," *The New York Times*, March 5, 1997.

[48] "Ugandan Rebel Activity Erupts In Fighting; Religious Fundamentalism One Cause," CNN World Report, February 20, 1997..

[49] "Uganda - Africa's Pearl: Trade On, and Damn the 'Mosquitoes,' " *The Guardian*, July 9, 1997.

This presents us with a familiar story; after all, the violence of "religious fanatics" appears, at first glance, to offer an explanation for the violence in northern Uganda. But as the children's testimonies demonstrate, to view the Lord's Resistance Army as "Christian fundamentalists" is a misleading oversimplification.

As Roger Winter of the U.S. Committee for Refugees notes, "too often outsiders assume that instability and violence in this region of Africa are endemic, as if they were part of the natural disorder."[50] But such journalistic oversimplifications promote a kind of passivity in the face of horrors: if Africa, or the Acholi, are just "like that," then efforts to resolve the conflict are inevitably in vain. Such an assumption, moreover, does a great disservice to the many thousands who suffer at the hands of the Lord's Resistance Army.

A History of Ethnic Violence

The background section of this report briefly described the way in which British colonial practices led to uneven economic development in Uganda, with southern Uganda becoming more prosperous than the north. This socio-economic division hardened as a result of the ethnic violence that characterized Uganda's post-independence decades, and that often fell out along north/south lines.

At independence in 1962, northerner Milton Obote became Uganda's first president. Obote, a northerner himself (a Langi), inherited the colonial army with its high percentage of northerners (especially Langi and Acholi). Obote's government lasted for nine years, until Obote was overthrown by army commander Idi Amin in 1971.

Amin, though a northerner like Obote, came from the West Nile region of Uganda. According to Thomas Ofcansky, a historian of the period, "Amin feared the influence of the Acholi and Langi, groups that dominated the armed forces."[51] A.B.K. Kasozi, the author of The Social Origins of Violence in Uganda, describes Amin's response to this perceived threat: "Amin brutally eliminated most of . . . the Langi and Acholi" in the army. They were replaced primarily by soldiers with ethnic and cultural links to Amin. [52] Amii Omara-Otunnu, author of Politics and the Military in Uganda, observes that "most of those who were massacred by Amin

---

[50] Roger Winter, U.S. Committee for Refugees, testimony before the African Affairs Subcommittee of the United States Senate Foreign Relations Subcommittee, May 15, 1997.

[51] Ofcansky, *Uganda: Tarnished Pearl of Africa*, p. 42-43.

[52] Kasozi, *The Social Origins of Violence in Uganda*, 1964-1985, p. 111.

were Acholi and Langi . . . . The killing of people mostly from those two ethnic groups had the effect of dividing the country."[53]

Amin himself was ultimately ousted by a coalition of forces that included Tanzanian government troops, supporters of former president Obote, and the followers of Yoweri Museveni, at that time a guerrilla leader. After defeating Amin in 1979, the alliance first put in place several compromise leaders, all from the south of Uganda. None of these leaders lasted for very long, and in May 1980, Milton Obote returned to the presidency.[54]

According to Kasozi and Omara-Otunno, Obote's return to power also restored the Acholi and Langi to dominance within Uganda's military, and heralded the beginning of another period of widespread violence. Yoweri Museveni's guerrilla National Resistance Army (dominated by southerners and westerners) sought to topple Obote by force, and the International Committee of the Red Cross ultimately estimated that fighting in Uganda's Luwero triangle region left several hundred thousand dead. The bulk of the dead were civilians.[55]

Already weakened by the National Resistance Army's successes, Obote finally fell in a coup staged by Acholi army leaders. On July 27, 1985, the coup brought General Tito Lutwa Okello, an Acholi, into power as head of state. Museveni's guerrilla National Resistance Army continued to fight the new Okello government, however, and on January 26, 1986, the National Resistance Army took Kampala, and Okello's Acholi soldiers retreated north, to the Acholi home districts of Gulu and Kitgum. Some of the soldiers crossed the Sudanese border, to take refuge with Acholi who lived in southern Sudan.

Paulinus Nyeko of Human Rights Focus observes that after Museveni's victory, many Acholi feared that Museveni's army would seek revenge on the Acholi ex-soldiers for their acts under previous governments.[56] The undisciplined actions of many National Resistance Army soldiers added to Acholi anxiety. Nyeko describes his memories of that period:

> National Resistance Army soldiers would do all they could to make things difficult here [in Gulu and Kitgum]. They would

---

[53] Omara-Otunnu, *Politics and the Military in Uganda*, p. 104.

[54] Ofcansky, *Uganda*, chapter 3.

[55] Ibid., p. 55.

[56] Human Rights Watch interview, Gulu, May 30, 1997.

defecate in water supplies, and in the mouths of slaughtered animals. They would tie people's hands behind their backs so tightly that people would be left paralyzed. They went into villages, and took guns by force. They looted Acholi cattle, and did nothing to prevent [cattle raiders from the Karamajong district] from stealing the rest. Over three million head of cattle were soon lost, and it made the people embittered.[57]

One further event sparked the beginnings of the Acholi rebellion: the National Resistance Army high command issued a directive over Radio Uganda, calling on Acholi ex-soldiers to report to Mbuya army headquarters within ten days. Nyeko observes that to many Acholi, this order was frighteningly reminiscent of the radio order that presaged one of Idi Amin's massacres of Acholi soldiers, and it inspired many additional Acholi ex-soldiers to leave Uganda to join their comrades who had fled to Sudan: "The order was just like in Amin's days," says Nyeko. "The Acholi boys said to each other, 'This time we are not going to die like chickens. Let us go to Sudan and join our brothers, and fight to save the Acholi.'"[58]

The Acholi ex-soldiers in Sudan soon joined forces with others opposed to Museveni's new government, including many Obote supporters and some of Amin's men. A rebel alliance was formed, calling itself the Uganda People's Defense Army (UPDA—not to be confused with the UPDF, the current name of the Ugandan government army). The UPDA made its first incursions into Uganda in August 1986. These rebel attacks focused on traditional military targets, not on civilians; indeed, the UPDA began by enjoying substantial support among the Acholi.

The Holy Spirit Movement

The UPDA was a coalition force made up of rebel factions with widely varying motives and histories, united only by their opposition to Museveni. In early November of 1986, Alice Lakwena, an Acholi healer and prophet, was given command of a UPDA battalion that came to be called the Holy Spirit Mobile Force. This force proved, briefly, to be a serious military threat to the National Resistance Army, and although its military potency was short-lived, it ultimately evolved into the Lord's Resistance Army, which causes so much bloodshed today.

---

[57] Human Rights Watch interview, Gulu, May 30, 1997.

[58] Ibid.

Alice Lakwena's Holy Spirit Movement began as a peaceful group, and understanding its origins requires a brief description of religious beliefs among the Acholi. Traditional Acholi religion included a belief in jogi (singular form: jok), which is probably best translated as "power": the jogi were the supernatural powers which could affect humanity. Jogi could be good or ill: the ancestors' jogi could assist their descendants, but also harm them, when angered. Chiefdom jogi, worked with by legitimate chiefs, was a force that fostered the well-being of the community, but the jok worked with by witches was harmful. As anthropologist Heike Behrend notes:

> In rituals different jogi were approached and appeased. . . . The
> different jogi cannot be understood as belonging either to the
> political or the religious sphere. They belong to both and have
> to be perceived along other lines. In Acholi thought the powers
> of different jogi were opposingly used in either the public or the
> private sphere and were regarded as being either productive,
> life-giving, or destructive, death-bringing. The power of a jok
> used for personal gain in private and for destruction constituted
> witchcraft, while the same power used in public for legitimate
> ends belonged to the chief and the priest.[59]

As the Acholi encountered colonialism and other unfamiliar forces and events, new jok were identified: Jok Allah, the jok of "Arabness;" Jok Rumba, the jok of "Europeaness," Jok Marin, the jok of "armyness;" Jok Rubanga, the jok causing tuberculosis of the spine, and so on. Many of these jogi generated cults of affliction, in which people sought to propitiate the jok with the power to cause those misfortunes they hoped to avoid.[60]

Christian missionaries sought to impose a Christian matrix onto the pre-existing belief system, and this led to a certain amount of confusion: not familiar with the complexity of the Acholi understanding of jogi, missionaries (rather arbitrarily, it seems) gave the Christian God the name of Jok Rubanga, which was thought by Acholi to be the jok responsible for spinal tuberculosis. As Christianity gained sway, new jogi emerged, such as Jok Jesus and the jok of the

---

[59] Heike Behrend, "Is Alice Lakwena a Witch?" in Hanson and Twaddle, eds., *Changing Uganda* (London: James Currie, 1991), p. 173.

[60] Behrend, p. 174.

Virgin Mary, and these Christian jogi became known as tipu, the Acholi term for the ghost of a dead relative. The Holy Spirit was translated as Tipu Maleng.

As Jok Rubanga became increasingly associated with the benevolent powers of the Christian god, other jogi came to be viewed as Satan's associates, and anyone working with them was presumed to be a witch. On the other hand, someone working with or possessed by a tipu, associated with Christianity, could be a healer and a prophet. Such healer/prophets sometimes drew large followings. Their relationship with the established churches was uneasy: on the one hand, such healer/prophets often identified themselves as Christians; on the other hand, much about their practices owed little to modern Christian doctrine.[61]

Alice Lakwena began her career as a healer and a prophet. She claimed to be possessed by the lakwena from whom she took her appellation; "lakwena" means messenger, and according to Alice, the lakwena possessing her was the tipu of an Italian who had died near the source of the Nile during the First World War. With his aid, Alice began to cure people of various diseases. As a healer, she attracted a great deal of support among the Acholi.

When the Acholi appeared to be threatened by Museveni's National Resistance Army, Alice evolved from a simple healer into a military leader, and she succeeded in getting UPDA commanders to provide her with weapons and soldiers. One of her early followers explained her transformation:

> The Lakwena appeared in Acholi because of the plan drawn by Y. Museveni and his government to kill all the male youths in Acholi as a revenge . . . so the Lakwena was sent to save the male youth . . . . The good Lord who sent the Lakwena decided to change his work from that of a doctor to that of a military commander for one simple reason: it is useless to cure a man today only that he be killed tomorrow. So it became an obligation on his part to stop the bloodshed before continuing his work as a doctor.[62]

For Alice, the roles of healer and military leader were inextricably bound together. In addition to leading soldiers into battle, Alice promised to cleanse the Acholi of the evil spirits and witchcraft that had caused so much trouble in the first place; this cleansing would ultimately lead to a new period of peace and prosperity.

---

[61] Behrend, pp. 175-76.

[62] Behrend, p. 165.

According to her followers, the Lakwena's appearance in Acholiland was "by no means accidental . . . . [T]he Acholi. . . have been notorious for murder, raping, looting, etc. , etc. It was therefore planned by God to help the Acholi to be converted [from] the evil ways of life to Godfearing and loving people. . . . "[63] Alice's soldiers had to undergo initiation rites in which they burned their old clothes and any magic charms, and swore by the Bible that they would no longer practice any form of sorcery or witchcraft. They would then be "anointed with shea oil and made holy." [64]

By all accounts, Alice Lakwena's Holy Spirit Movement was a genuinely popular millenarian uprising. "Alice united people," says Alphonse Owiny-Dollo, the Minister of State for the North. "She was magnetic and charismatic, and appeared as someone who could get rid of bad elements and cure the illness in society. People supported her. "[65] Cathy Watson, a former BBC journalist who interviewed many of Lakwena's followers, agrees: "Non-Acholi weren't the only ones to blame the Acholi for the Luwero atrocities. The Acholis blamed themselves, and felt that they were sinful. Following Alice was a way to purify yourself, and become free of that. Alice inspired hope and joy, and she had these wonderful millenarian promises."[66] Livingstone Sewanyana, a Kampala human rights activist, says that "People believed in Alice. She had power."[67]

Lakwena's Holy Spirit forces inflicted violence on the civilian population as well as on National Resistance Army soldiers, but this violence was justified by her followers as part of the struggle to get the Acholi to turn from their "evil ways of life." In particular, the Holy Spirit Movement fought against witches, sorcerers, and all others perceived to be working with spirits, for whatever ostensible purpose. As Minister Alphonse Owiny-Dollo explains it, "Lakwena's forces killed, but her followers accepted the killings as a form of severe punishment. Wrongdoers among the Acholi were being killed. And if you were only killing witches and

---

[63] Behrend., pp. 166-67.

[64] Behrend, p. 167.

[65] Human Rights Watch interview, Kampala, May 20, 1997.

[66] Human Rights Watch interview, Kampala, May 26, 1997.

[67] Human Rights Watch interview, Kampala, May 26, 1997.

such like, this was not evil."[68]   Although thousands joined Alice of their own accord, the Holy Spirit Movement's military wing also abducted many people: but abductions, too, were justified as being for the good of the abductee.

Alice promised her soldiers that when they were anointed with shea butter oil, bullets would bounce harmlessly off their chests. Her soldiers also had to obey a complicated set of rules: drinking, smoking, stealing, and quarreling were all forbidden, as was taking cover in battle. Breaking any of these rules might lead to death in battle.[69]

Inspired by Alice, the soldiers of the Holy Spirit Movement inflicted a number of embarrassing defeats on the National Resistance Army, who were at first nonplussed by the sight of thousands of poorly armed soldiers streaming forward, making no attempt to take cover. In January 1987, the Holy Spirit Movement's soldiers made it as far south as Jinja, only sixty miles from Kampala. At this point, however, superior technology won the day: Lakwena, Owiny Dollo says dryly, "thought she could use stones against modern weapons—it didn't work."[70] With countless dead, the military wing of the Holy Spirit Movement appeared to be utterly destroyed.[71]

After the defeat at Jinja, Lakwena herself fled to Kenya, where she is said to remain today. Exhausted and demoralized, many of her remaining soldiers surrendered, and those who had been abducted took the opportunity to escape. Museveni and his soldiers continued to fight against the remnants of the Holy Spirit Movement and the UPDA rebel alliance, but at the same time they offered an amnesty to any rebels who surrendered. They promised to reintegrate into the army and civil service those rebels who stopped fighting, and they kept their promise; the combination of Lakwena's defeat and the lure of peace and a return to normal life led many rebels to leave the bush voluntarily. By early 1989, the UPDA had virtually ceased to exist.[72]

---

[68] Human Rights Watch interview with Hon. Alphonse Owiny-Dollo, Minister of State for the North, Kampala, May 20, 1997.

[69] Behrend, "Is Alice Lakwena a Witch?" pp. 168-69.

[70] Human Rights Watch interview, Kampala, May 20, 1997.

[71] A.G.G. Gingyera-Pinyewa, *Northern Uganda in National Politics* (Kampala: Fountain Publishers, 1992), pp. 21-22.

[72] Ofcansky, *Uganda*, pp. 63-64.

The Emergence of the Lord's Resistance Army

But if many of the UPDA soldiers were fairly quickly talked out of the bush, Lakwena's more dedicated followers were not so easily budged. The UPDA soldiers, after all, had never been a very cohesive force: they had been bound together only by a shared opposition to Museveni. A remnant of the Holy Spirit Movement, led by the young Joseph Kony (he was only about twenty at the time), remained in the bush. Kony, who is said to be a relative of Alice, claims to share (or to have inherited) Alice's spiritual powers. Although the rituals and beliefs of Kony's followers differed slightly from those of Alice's followers, Kony and Alice appear to have worked in close cooperation before Alice's defeat and flight. He would dress like Alice during certain rituals, and he and Alice apparently performed many rituals together.[73]

Kony's group underwent a number of name changes, but eventually began to call itself the Lord's Resistance Army.[74] For several years after Alice's defeat, the Lord's Resistance Army continued to harass government installations and those civilians seen as wrongdoers or government collaborators. At some point—most observers place it as early 1991—their tactics shifted, and they began large-scale attacks on civilian targets, including schools and clinics. Abductions, especially of children, were also stepped up.[75]

Little information is publicly available about this phase of the Lord's Resistance Army's activities. In 1991, the Museveni government responded to its inability to defeat the rebels by sealing off the northern districts of Gulu, Kitgum, Lira and Apac for "intensive military operations" against what they viewed as "gun-toting and panga-wielding thugs-cum-rebels."[76] During "Operation North,"

---

[73] Several anthropologists did a significant amount of research on Lakwena and Kony during this early period (1985-88), and readers wanting a fuller discussion of the Holy Spirit Movement and Kony's early leadership should consult the work of Heike Behrend, cited above, and Tim Allen, "Understanding Alice: Uganda's Holy Spirit Movement in Context," *Africa*, Volume 61, Number 3, 1991, pp. 370-99.

[74] For convenience, we will refer to Kony's followers as the Lord's Resistance Army from this point on, although this name is somewhat anachronistic when applied to Kony's group during the late eighties and early nineties.

[75] Gingyera-Pinyewa, *Northern Uganda*, p. 20.

[76] Ibid.

there was a total press blackout, and the government forbade communication or physical movement between the sealed provinces and the rest of the country.[77]

According to Acholi members of parliament, Operation North was a tactical and human rights disaster: "Operation North. . . created more problems than it solved. . . . Private radio communications [methods] were removed from institutions and NGOs; there was massive arrest of civic leaders; the press was not allowed in the area and all members of parliament from the area were forcefully evicted/barred from Gulu, Kitgum, Apac and Lira."[78] During the operation, the government resorted to "protected camps" not unlike those creating so much suffering today, and many have alleged that National Resistance Army soldiers committed various atrocities. The Acholi Parliamentary Group, for instance, charges that:

> People were herded into camps without food, health care, etc.
> for days at various locations purportedly for screening. Many
> people died and there were human rights abuses all over. Some
> innocent civilians were buried alive in Bucoro, while others were
> shot, crops in the fields were destroyed by the National
> Resistance Army. The NRA Mobile Battalion nicknamed
> 'GUNGA' committed homosexual acts even with very old men,
> raped wives, mothers and daughters in the presence of their
> families. This painted a terrible picture of the National
> Resistance Army. At the same time, Kony had also started
> abducting, raping and killing of innocent people using pangas.[79]

Like previous National Resistance Army efforts, Operation North failed to wipe out Kony's rebels. Arguably, the Lord's Resistance Army became even more of a problem as time passed: the rebels stepped up their attacks on civilian targets, and spent less and less time attacking government installations.

In 1994, attempts were made to start negotiations between the government and the rebels. For a while, the prospects for peace looked bright: "UPDF guys and

---

[77] Ibid.

[78] Acholi Parliamentary Group, "Submission to the Parliamentary Committee on Defense and Internal Affairs Investigating the Northern Rebellion with a View to Bringing it to a Speedy End," date uncertain, but probably December 1996 or January 1997, pp. 5-6.

[79] Ibid.

Kony's men were drinking together in bars," says Paulinus Nyeko at Gulu Human Rights Focus.[80] But for some reason, the negotiations fell apart. The government claims that the rebels were not serious about peace, while government critics claim that the government lured rebel leaders to peace talks and then staged an ambush, killing several rebel commanders.[81] For whatever reason, the negotiations failed, and the violence continued.

The Role of Sudan

The most recent phase of the conflict in the north began about two years ago, when Sudan started to provide substantial aid to the Lord's Resistance Army. Equipped with machine guns and land mines in place of pangas and rifles, the Lord's Resistance Army's ability to terrorize and kill increased many times over. It seems clear that since 1995, the number of people abducted and killed by the Lord's Resistance Army has dramatically increased.

Although the government of Sudan denies that it provides military aid to the Lord's Resistance Army, these denials cannot be taken seriously.[82] Many of the children and adults abducted by the Lord's Resistance Army escape from Lord's Resistance Army camps in Sudan, or surrender to the rebel Sudanese People's Liberation Army (SPLA), which then turns them over to the Ugandan army (now called the Ugandan People's Defense Force, or UPDF—not to be confused with the defunct rebel alliance, the UPDA). The escapees recall the arrival in Kony's camp of heavy trucks driven by "Arabs" in Sudanese army uniform, bearing food and weapons. Some escapees report that seriously injured rebels were airlifted to hospitals in Khartoum.

---

[80] Human Rights Watch interview, Gulu, May 30, 1997.

[81] Human Rights Watch interview, Ron and Pam Ferguson, Mennonite Central Committee, Kampala, May 31, 1997.

[82] In the wake of the abduction of thirty girls from St. Mary's School in Aboke, the Ugandan government began to negotiate with Sudan for the return of the girls, who were believed to have been taken across the Sudanese border by the Lord's Resistance Army. The Sudanese government eventually permitted a delegation that included the deputy headmistress of St. Mary's and a representative of the Concerned Parents of Aboke, to visit an LRA camp in Sudan, under Sudanese government auspices. Although the Sudanese government insisted that it knew nothing about the fate of the Aboke abductees, the tour of the LRA camp further undermines the Sudanese government's assertion that it does not support or control the LRA.

The Sudanese government has a dual motive for supporting the Lord's Resistance Army. First, the Lord's Resistance Army is used by the Sudanese government to fight in its increasingly desperate war against the rebel Sudanese People's Liberation Army (SPLA). Second, Sudan has long accused the Ugandan government of aiding the SPLA. Sudan's support for the Lord's Resistance Army is thus a form of retaliation. While the Lord's Resistance Army constitutes little serious threat to the Museveni government, it is nonetheless an embarrassment and a serious drain on the national budget.

There is, of course, an apparent irony in Sudan's support for the Lord's Resistance Army: the Sudanese government is militantly Islamic, while the Lord's Resistance Army is at least ostensibly Christian. But over time, it seems clear that the beliefs and practices of Kony and his followers have changed: in 1987, Kony's group was closely identified with Alice Lakwena, and like Lakwena, Kony appears to have enjoyed substantial popular support among the Acholi. Huge crowds would gather to hear him preach.[83] By May 1997, when we conducted most of our interviews, the testimony of the children we met suggested that many of the rituals common in Lakwena's time had been abandoned or were only sporadically followed. Many children also reported rebel practices that appear to have been adopted from Islam: for instance, the rebels pray while facing Mecca, respect Friday as a holy day, and forbid the keeping of pigs.[84]

Why the Conflict Persists

The uneven economic development of north and south and the history of ethnic violence have cast a long shadow over Uganda. For the Acholi people, the legacy of the decades following independence has been one of demoralization and distrust. This climate of hopelessness has provided the rebel Lord's Resistance Army with ideal conditions for sowing discord and terror.

The rebels themselves claim that they will fight until they overthrow the government of Yoweri Museveni. In the absence of a clearly reliable official spokesperson for the rebels, their more specific political grievances can only be

---

[83] Human Rights Watch interview, Cathy Watson, Kampala, May 26, 1997.

[84] According to one news report, Joseph Kony recently converted to Islam at the behest of the Sudanese government. See Emmy Alio, "Uganda: Kony Converts to Islam," *Africa News*, July 31, 1997.

pieced together from the reports of escapees.[85] The rebels appear to view Museveni as an illegitimate leader because of his refusal to allow multi-party elections, his alleged strategy of keeping the north poor and under-developed, and his alleged dislike and mistreatment of the Acholi. The rebels still insist that they are obeying the orders of the Holy Spirit, and there can be little doubt that religious rituals, of however eclectic a nature, are important in rebel life. The rebels continue to claim that they must root out "misbehavior" and offenses among the Acholi as part of their effort to overthrow the government and turn Uganda into a "paradise."

It is tempting to speculate on whether the rebels "really" believe any of this—to what extent are the rebels true believers, and to what extent is religion being cynically manipulated for unrelated ends? But this may not be an entirely

---

[85] A number of expatriate Acholi have at varying times come forward and claimed to be spokepeople for the Lord's Resistance Army, but the utter lack of agreement between their statements and the actions of the rebels casts serious doubt on their ability to speak for the LRA. Government officials, journalists and local activists all agree that the various LRA "spokesmen" cannot be assumed to have any real authority within the LRA, and may, indeed, have no connection at all to the LRA

For instance, at a recent conference of Acholi leaders held at the University of London, a paper was given by Dr. James Obita, who claims to be the Lord's Resistance Army Secretary for External Affairs and Mobilisation. According to Dr. Obite, the aims of the LRA are: "a) To remove dictatorship and stop the oppression of our people; b) To fight for the immediate restoration of competitive multi party democracy in Uganda; c)To see an end to gross violation of human rights and dignity of Ugandans; d) To ensure the restoration of peace and security in Uganda; e) To ensure unity, sovereignty and economic prosperity beneficial to all Ugandans; f) To bring to an end to the repressive policy of deliberate marginalization of groups of people who may not agree with the NRA ideology."

Dr. Obita insisted that the LRA does not abduct children or kill civilians: "It is . . . not the policy of the LRM/A to abduct or force people to join its ranks . . . . We are usually shocked and puzzled when we hear government allegations that the LRA are massacring civilians in the villages of northern Uganda. LRA has no programmes or intentions of killing the very people they are supposed to defend and protect." Obita atributed such atrocities to government soldiers disguised as rebels: "The aim for these atrocities by the UPDF and the shifting of the blames for them on the LRA is intended to discredit the LRA and simultaneously frighten and anger the civilian population of northern Uganda with the hope of turning them against LRA." Dr James Alfred Obita, Secretary for External Affairs and Mobilisation, Lord's Resistance Movement/Army, "A Case For National Reconciliation, Peace, Democracy And Economic Prosperity For All Ugandans." Paper Presented At Kacoke Madit, London, April 5-6, 1997. This and other documents of Obita's have been disseminated via the world-wide web at http://www.columbia.edu/~bo23/obita-km.htm.

meaningful question. For one thing, the question assumes that "the rebels" are a monolithic force. It is impossible to know how many of the rebel commanders are left over from the days of Lakwena's Holy Spirit movement, and it is also impossible to know just what motivates them to fight.

What evidence we have suggests that while Kony's control over the Lord's Resistance Army is near total, a great number—perhaps even a large majority—of the "rebels" are abducted children, rather than adults who voluntarily joined Kony. Terrified and indoctrinated, the children participate in atrocities along with the adults. Although some of the children obey their captors only out of a wholly non-spiritual fear, some of them certainly believe what they are told about the Holy Spirit, and some of them grow to adulthood among the rebels, and cease to imagine having any other identity.

In the end, some of the rebels probably commit atrocities out of the sincere belief that they are obeying the Holy Spirit's orders to eliminate wrongdoers within the Acholi community; some probably participate in atrocities only because they fear being killed if they refuse; some may literally be unable to imagine any other life, and some may be acting solely to increase their personal power and prestige. And some, of course, may act out of a combination of all of those motives.

Needless to say, despite all Lord's Resistance Army claims to be fighting on behalf of the Acholi, and despite whatever popular Acholi support Kony may have had in the late 1980s, it seems overwhelmingly clear that today the Acholi people regard Lord's Resistance Army activities as an unmitigated evil. Hardly a family remains untouched by the violence, and nearly all of our interviewees, both Acholi and non-Acholi, vehemently denied the idea that Kony's rebellion is in any sense a popular movement. According to Paulinus Nyeko, some Acholi civilians believe that Kony does possess spiritual powers, but they see him as having wrongly usurped them from Alice Lakwena: "In the villages, many people think the spirit which had possessed Alice has moved on to Kony, and that he uses it for ill where Alice used it for good. People say that Kony will only lose his powers if Alice comes back from Kenya."[86]

In late May 1997, the wife of an Anglican bishop who had been an outspoken critic of rebel atrocities died when her car hit a land mine; some saw this as further evidence of Kony's spiritual power to punish his enemies.[87] But fear of

---

[86] Human Rights Watch interview, Gulu, May 30, 1997.

[87] Human Rights Watch interview, Sister Bruna Barollo, Camboni Sisters, Kampala, May 26, 1997.

Kony's alleged supernatural powers does not translate into Acholi support for the rebels. "We Acholi are the ones who bear the brunt of the suffering," says Alphonse Owiny-Dollo, Minister of State for the North. "It is our children who are being abducted and killed. Any sympathy people might have had for Kony is long over."[88] Daniel Omara-Atuba, the MP for Lira, observes that "there is no sensible leader in the north who supports Kony. He is a killer, and the people are tired of him."[89] Livingstone Okello-Okello, MP for Kitgum, was equally clear: "The rebels have zero support. There is nobody in Acholi who has not lost a relative. Since 1991, I don't think anyone has voluntarily joined the rebels. Some people believe Kony has power, but they think it is witchcraft, not the power of God."[90]

Many Ugandan government officials insist that Kony himself is motivated neither by religious beliefs nor by any real desire to overthrow the government, but by nothing more complicated than greed. "I believe that Kony himself gets everything he wants from this war," said James Kazini, the commander of the Uganda People's Defense Force Fourth Division in Gulu. "Because he helps fight the SPLA, he gets aid from Sudan. So he has women, power, a car."[91] Alphonse Owiny-Dollo articulated a similar theory:

> Kony is just a villain. He has something like twenty wives, and the SPLA says that his camp is like a palace built of grass thatch huts. Back in Uganda, Kony would not get that respect. And so he has to keep abducting children—it's simple. Without abducting children, Kony would have no army. If he had no army, he couldn't fight the SPLA. If he couldn't fight the SPLA, he would get no more money from Sudan—without soldiers, without abductees, Sudan would drop him, and he would then be nowhere.[92]

---

[88] Human Rights Watch interview, Kampala, May 26, 1997.

[89] Human Rights Watch interview, Kampala, June 3, 1997.

[90] Human Rights Watch interview, Kampala, June 2, 1997.

[91] Human Rights Watch interview, Gulu, May 30, 1997.

[92] Human Rights Watch interview, Kampala, May 26, 1997.

President Museveni shares this view of Kony:

> Kony is not fighting for political aims but for a style of living
> that he cannot afford through legal toil. Kony has now got
> pick-ups given to him by the Sudan government; scores of
> wives; buildings in townships and trading centers in Acholi, and
> other forms of property. He wants to remain in Sudan or in the
> mountains taking chickens from the villagers. Settling down to
> work for a chicken takes discipline and labor. If people who do
> not want to work happen to have the gun, until you control them
> they will use guns to achieve their ends . . . . In other words,
> they are parasites on society. If Kony and his group were
> fighting for political power, why should they defile and rape
> children? Why would they mutilate civilians? They should
> concentrate on the government and army in their attacks. They
> are after wealth through lawless means.[93]

The government has repeatedly characterized the rebels as mere "bandits"
and thugs, and insisted that with only a few small bands remaining in the Ugandan
countryside, the rebels are on the verge of being permanently defeated by the
Uganda People's Defense Force. In a recent interview with the Guardian, Ugandan
finance minister Jehoash Mayanja Nkangi dismissed the rebels as "mosquitoes."[94]
In late April, President Museveni informed Parliament that "the remnants of
Kony's group have broken into small groups that are being picked off one by one,
or they are surrendering in droves."[95]
But events at the time of Museveni's speech starkly contrasted with this
optimism: throughout April and May, there were several hundred thousand
displaced people in Gulu and Kitgum, and new abductions and attacks almost every
day. Although about 13,000 Uganda People's Defense Force soldiers (a mixture

---

[93] Yoweri Museveni, address at the opening of parliament, April 28, 1997.

[94] "Uganda - Africa's Pearl: Trade On, and Damn the 'Mosquitoes,' " *Guardian*,
July 9, 1997.

[95] Museveni, address to parliament, April 28, 1997.

of regulars and militia) are stationed in Gulu and Kitgum,[96] and the government reportedly spends an estimated 800 million Ugandan shillings a day (roughly, U.S. $800,000) on expenses associated with the conflict,[97] the war in the north has now dragged on for more than ten years.

Commander Kazini attributes the government's failure to wipe out the rebels in part to the existence of collaborators among the Acholi civilians. Several children told us that civilians do help the rebels at times, but for the most part, civilians have no real alternative. "The civilian population is caught in the middle," explains Omaru Atubo, the MP for Lira. "Basically they are forced to cooperate with whoever controls their area at any given time."[98] Jim Mugungu, a journalist, observes that "people collaborate out of fear. It's not because they support the rebels. It's because they don't want to be killed or mutilated. If they defy the rebels, the UPDF won't protect them—so they have no choice."[99]

Angelina Atyoum, whose daughter was abducted by the rebels last October, poses the civilian dilemma starkly:

> If the rebels abduct your child, how can you think of the rebels with anything but horror? Kony is an evil madman, and you don't want the rebels to go on committing these atrocities, killing and taking children from mothers, forcing our children themselves to kill for their very survival. But now: your own child is living as a rebel. So if the rebels come through and demand food or information, it is not only your fear for yourself, you think also of your child, and hope that your own child is not hungry. So perhaps you help the rebels.
>
> This is what many Acholi parents in the villages must feel. The Acholi are helpless, their problems have crushed them. The

---

[96] Human Rights Watch interview, Commander James Kazini, UPDF Fourth Division, Gulu, May 30, 1997.

[97] Human Rights Watch interview, Paulinus Nyeko, Gulu, May 30, 1997.

[98] Human Rights Watch interview, Kampala, June 3, 1997.

[99] Human Rights Watch interview, Jim Mugungu, Monitor newspaper, Kampala, June 3, 1997.

rebels come, they are harsh; the UPDF comes, and they are harsh too. Who should they trust?[100]

Indeed, as the war drags on, many of the casualties are children. Norbert Mao, MP for Gulu, points out that:

> The rebel commanders rarely face the UPDF themselves. It is the children who they send to the front. So in fighting with the UPDF, it is the children who are mown down by the bullets. Kony pushes the hand of the government army against the children. Children are sent to the front, and they die. So Kony is driven to abduct still more children to replace them—the border with Sudan is long, and the UPDF cannot police it, so Kony has an inexhaustible supply of children to abduct. So what we have is a terrible cycle: Kony abducts children, they die in fighting with the UPDF, so he abducts more, and they are killed, and so on.[101]

Although some children are killed while actively fighting against government forces, others—including new captives—are simply caught in the crossfire. Unarmed and often tied up—often tied to a long chain of other captives—the newest captives are extremely vulnerable during rebel confrontations with government forces. Angelina Atyoum, whose daughter is still missing, sums up the problem: "I want the rebels to be defeated. But if you go against the rebels militarily, you are causing the death of our children. The children are caught in the crossfire. As a parent, how can I support that?"[102]

---

[100] Human Rights Watch interview, Angelina Atyoum, Concerned Parents of Aboke, Aboke, May 28, 1997.

[101] Human Rights Watch interview, Kampala, June 2, 1997.

[102] Human Rights Watch interview, Aboke, May 28, 1997. The Ugandan government is committed to defeating the Lord's Resistance Army through military means. It should be noted that most Acholi elected leaders, along with NGOs like Gulu Human Rights Focus and the Acholi Development Association, oppose this policy on the grounds that it has led to excessive loss of civilan lives. These leaders and organizations urge a negotiated end to the conflict.

Many Acholi see their situation as hopeless: whatever happens, they suffer. "When the government fights the rebels lately, mostly it is local defense units [the militia] being sent to fight, not the regular UPDF soldiers," said Paulinus Nyeko. "Since it is mostly Acholi in the local defense units, and they go to fight Acholi rebels, many of whom are abducted children, what we have now is Acholi fighting Acholi children. If this conflict does not end we will have none of us left."[103]

The war's long duration tends to fuel Acholi fears that the conflict is somehow part of a government plan to take revenge on them for the atrocities of the past. "People are very frightened," says Paulinus Nyeko:

> They think that this war is part of a plan to exterminate the Acholi: the government just lets Kony loose among us like a beast in the jungle, and stands by while we all kill each other. This may sound like paranoia to an outsider, but remember the tragedy of Uganda: this is the sort of thing that has already happened in the past. So many people are ready to believe that it is happening again.[104]

Although few northern leaders countenance such extreme views, many charge that the government lacks the political will to bring the conflict to a speedy end. "This is a proxy war, with the SPLA fighting Museveni's war, and Kony fighting the government of Sudan's war," says Lira MP Daniel Omara Atubo.[105] "The Acholi are the sacrificial lambs in a conflict between Uganda and Sudan," says Andres Banya.[106] Gulu MP Norbert Mao agrees:

> What this is about is the conflict between Uganda and Sudan. As long as Sudan assists the Kony rebels, it will be almost impossible to destroy them; their bases are across the border, and they come into Uganda as guerrillas, they have heavy weapons.

---

[103] Human Rights Watch interview, Gulu, May 30, 1997.

[104] Ibid.

[105] Human Rights Watch, Kampala, June 3, 1997.

[106] Human Rights Watch interview, Andres Banya, Acholi Development Association, Kampala, June 2, 1997.

But Sudan will not stop helping the rebels unless Uganda stops helping the SPLA. And Museveni does not want to stop helping the SPLA. Meanwhile, people outside of the north shrug, and say, "Well, with these rebels it is Acholi killing Acholi—when they get tired, they will stop." It is a callousness that causes us to lose heart.[107]

Kitgum MP Livingstone Okello-Okello argues that the government finds the war in the north convenient as a cover for covert aid to allies in Zaire, Rwanda, Kenya and Burundi, as well as Sudan:

The war in the north is being used as a financial conduit to fund other wars. The amount allegedly being spent on the war in the north is vast, and in ten years we see no results. The money goes elsewhere. This is a poor country, and so you cannot say to parliament, "I want money to fight wars in other nations." But if you say, "We need money to fight the war in the north," then you get the money and no one can say anything more. And meanwhile, the Acholi die, and there is less money for social welfare and development all over.[108]

Norbert Mao sums up the view of most northern leaders:

In a way, it doesn't matter why the war doesn't end, whether it's because there are those in the army who hate the Acholi, or because the army is incompetent and corrupt, or because funds and resources are being diverted to other places. Whatever the reason, the fact is that ten years have gone by and things have gotten worse, not better. Our children are being taken, and the government is not protecting them.[109]

---

[107] Human Rights Watch interview, Kampala, June 2, 1997.

[108] Human Rights Watch interview, Kampala, June 2, 1997.

[109] Human Rights Watch interview, Kampala, June 2, 1997.

V. CONCLUSION

The first thing to do is find a way to protect our children.
Otherwise, you may shout on top of the mountain, but it will do
no good if they can still take our children.

- Dr. Matthew Lukwiya, Lacor Hospital, Gulu[110]

Wer Pak Pa Acholi :

Song of Praise for the Acholi:

Acholo wa do Acholi wa yee
Lotino Acholi gucung pi' in
Acholi wa do piny me kuc
Lotino Acholi gube tiyo pi in

Acholi children,
Stand for the land.
Our Acholi land is a place of happiness
And the children will work for the land.

Lobo Acholi ceko cam mada
In Lacwec med tanga meri ba
Kum ngom man wa dano mere duc
Tanga ni omed mar ki kuk
Joo Acholi loko leb mupyee

Acholi land is very fertile
So you, God, add your blessing
On the land and the people who live in it.
Let your blessing also bring love and peace.
The people of Acholi speak a clear language

Lebbe ber ribo dano duc
Joo Acholi jollo dano weng
Man ber ribbo Uganda.

That unites all the people.
The people of Acholi welcome everybody
And this is good, for it unites Uganda.[111]

The children of northern Uganda are being denied their most fundamental rights by the rebels of the Lord's Resistance Army. Taken violently from their homes and families, the children are used as pack animals by the rebels, forced to carry heavy loads until some collapse from exhaustion. Those who collapse are killed. Children who try to escape are stabbed or clubbed to death, and the rebels force other captive children to mete out these grisly punishments. The children are forced to participate in other atrocities, as well, including the murder of civilians and the looting and destruction of homes and stores.

Once at the rebel camp in Sudan, the children must work for the rebels as virtual slaves. All children receive military training, and girls are given to rebel

---

[110] Human Rights Watch interview, Gulu, May 29, 1997.

[111] Song in Acholi Development Association brochure, 1997. Translated into English for Human Rights Watch by Ponsiano Ochero, UNICEF.

commanders as "wives." During fighting in Uganda and Sudan, rebel commanders force young chidren—some not even armed—to run to the front lines. The children are often not permitted to take cover, and many die in battle. The rebels keep the children obedient through frequent beatings, threats of death, and threats of retaliation against the children's family members.

The impact of the Lord's Resistance Army's brutal methods is not only felt by abducted children. The conflict in the north has led directly or indirectly to the deaths of many thousands of civilians, and to the complete devastation of Uganda's northern districts. Many roads are unsafe because of land mines and the danger of rebel ambushes, and many of the region's schools have been burnt down.

Hundreds of thousands of civilians have lost their homes and crops, and have obeyed the government's injunction to crowd into "protected camps" near government military installations. Conditions in the camps are atrocious. Lack of food, water, sanitary facilities and medical care has led to thousands of deaths from malnutrition and epidemic diseases, and continued rebel attacks on the protected camps themselves have led to still more deaths.

Children lucky enough to escape from the rebels may be held by government forces for excessively long periods of time before being reunited with family members or sent to a trauma counseling center. Some children do not receive adequate medical care while in the hands of the government soldiers, and conditions in the trauma counseling centers are also inadequate, with many children crowded into a small and poorly secured area. Despite poor conditions at the trauma counseling centers, which are funded entirely by international NGO's, many children fear returning home and being re-abducted by the rebels. Many more have been orphaned by the war; others may have living relatives, but do not know where to find them.

Although children are far from the only ones who are suffering as a result of the Lord's Resistance Army, it is unquestionably the very young who are suffering the most. As this report went to press, the abductions were still going on unabated. Even if the crisis ended tomorrow, the effects of the Lord's Resistance Army's atrocities will haunt Uganda for generations to come.

The Lord's Resistance Army should comply with its obligations under international humanitarian law, and the government of Uganda should take all possible steps to protect the rights of Ugandan children, as required by the Convention on the Rights of the Child. But the international community, too, has a tremendous responsibility to end the violation of children's rights in Uganda.

Graca Machel, the head of the 1996 United Nations Study on the Impact of Armed Conflict on Children, has noted:

> The crisis in the Great Lakes region of Africa is developing into a catastrophic human tragedy. Despite repeated warnings, despite increasing numbers of deaths, despite clear violations of children's rights, the international community has failed to act. . . . The protection and care of children in armed conflicts requires greater political will, continued vigilance, and increased cooperation.[112]

The children of Uganda see their own tragedy clearly, but without help, they are powerless to protect themselves.

Below are excerpts from some of the letters written to Human Rights Watch by Ugandan children:

Abigail, fifteen:

> What kind of world are we living in? Please, as you have a willing heart to help, please do! . . . Is this not so miserable? I ask for more help from you to bring peace and children's rights to our country. We want to have a voice in our country, to develop it, not destroy it.

Helen, sixteen:

> Would you encourage the government of Uganda to provide good security to all places in the North [and] make both the Ugandan government and the Sudanese government have a good relationship, through peace talks? I pray that you work more to find a way of restoring peace in our district, country and the entire world.

Grace, fourteen:

> Please! Please! Please! If you can bring back our brothers and sisters who are suffering in the bush I think it will be much better. . . I am here in school now but doing badly because I am

---

[112] Graca Machel, Statement to the Third Committee of the U.N. General Assembly, November 8, 1996.

thinking about my sister and brother who have been taken away
from school [by the rebels]. If I go home from school and I see
my parents, and how sad they are, I myself start to cry.

I have much more to tell you, but the more words I write, that is
the more sad I become.

Janet, fifteen:

There are thousands of young children the rebels have taken
from their parents, suffering. . . .There are many people without
a place to sleep or even anything to eat, but there is nothing
being done for them.

So to anyone who reads this, my question is: what can we say
and do for the thousands and thousands of young people. . . who
are still suffering in the bush with Kony Joseph, and for the
hundreds of people who die there day and night?

My question remains to the one who reads this and meditates
over it.

The children of Uganda are calling on the world to help. Let us not turn
our backs upon their appeals.

APPENDICES

APPENDIX A
Letters from the Aboke School Girls

The following testimonials were written in English by students of the St. Mary's school in Aboke, where 139 girls were abducted *en masse* by the Lord's Resistance Army in October 1996. Human Rights Watch visited the school in May 1997, and collected written testimonials from over one hundred students who were abducted. Selected testimonials are set forth below. The language is the girls' own, but has been lightly edited for clarity.

Student letter #1

It was surprising to me when I heard the way those people treat people. I didn't believe when I was told, until at last I came to see these things with my own eyes. I saw peoples' legs being cut with either a panga or an axe. I saw a young baby of a few months held in hand and beaten to death against a tree. I saw children of 10 years being taken into slavery. Innocent people were killed in a way that I never thought a human being could [act towards] another human being.

Imagine a very old man, that cannot even run, having his leg cut off while some people just step on him! However harsh you are, can't you sympathize on such an old, gray haired man? Whoever tries to escape, if they get that person, is killed by [being hit on] the head until the skull is just crushed bones. A girl of 12 years was killed while I was seeing blood flood on the ground. People's lips [were] being cut off and people's mouths were locked with padlocks. At times they cut the breasts off women.

Just feel within yourself, if you were the one seeing all these things taking place in your presence-- How would you feel? It is a feeling that for me I can't express, but it can lead to my death. If I think of these things I'm still affected. Maybe if my friends come back I will be relieved. This makes me question myself at times about: what is the world doing? Is this Kony so powerful? I have stayed with them [and] I saw evidence of no super power.

So I appeal to you, if possible, try your best. I pray that with God's help my friends will come back through your effort. However, if I think of them, at times I become senseless and my brain does not function well, for they were my great friends that I used to share everything with. I tell you, you cannot feel the pain of this suffering if you don't see it physically. If you only glance at it, a sword of sorrow will pierce your heart. I don't cry only for my friends but also [for] the other innocent children suffering in this mysterious slavery. In addition to that, some children have had their parents killed by the rebels and they are now displaced from their homes. They are now living like birds, depending on wild fruits.   On my God!   What on earth is it, that man today does not care for his fellow humans? Sincerely, even now [when] I write, I'm upset.

Furthermore the rebels are misusing girls.   You can find a girl of 12 years given to a man of 35 years as a wife and the man goes with the girl without feeling ashamed.   I'm telling things I saw happening with my own eyes, not just what I have been told.

I saw people returning from Sudan when I had not yet escaped; they were skin and bones with eyes.

A long time I spent with the rebels.   I cannot even tell the main aim in what they are doing. I don't know what you as an organization can do with these people. [Or] how fast you can reach to their help and rescue.   Otherwise this violence seems the contrary of everything we hope for on earth. I have talked through experience. How will Uganda remain a nation if this continues? Maybe it will be a nation of the dead, and not of the living.

Student letter #2
What I Experienced and Will Never Forget in Life

I am by name --, student of senior four, age 17. It was on October 9, 1996 when the Kony rebels appeared to break into our school. They entered the school by breaking the windows of our dormitory and then managed to enter the dormitory and open the door. They came in and switched the lights on. All of us were caught and tied up with ropes and [we] walked with them all night till we reached a certain very far village.

On the way we saw our Reverend Sister Rachele following us; she was with one of our teachers. They went to the rebel commander, asking him to release us, but the man was not interested in hearing our sister's words. A government plane came looking for the rebels and all of us were made to hide in the grass so that the pilot could not see us. After that, we continued moving with Sister following us. Then they made us sit down together.

The rebels selected 30 of us, then told Sister that she could go back with [the remaining girls.] But Sister insisted on telling the commander of the rebels to release all of us. The man said to Sister that if that was the case, he [would] take all 139 girls. Sister cried in front of the rebels to release all of us, but in vain. She was ready to go with the rebels on our behalf or even to die for us, but the rebels refused. Sister came and told us not to be afraid, not to fear anything because the Lord will be with us. Whatever suffering we may go through, the Almighty God [would] be with us. She gave us her rosary for praying in the bush. She left with the rest of the girls, but kept looking at us, because she could not really leave us behind. But all in vain.

We (thirty girls) slept in that village with the rebels and the next morning, we started moving. Every where that [we] moved, we always met ambushes and we only barely survived death from the gun shot, bombs etc. that they used for fighting with UPDF soldiers, here in Uganda. We nearly died crossing water: whether you drowned in the water or not, they could not care less. For example, I was shot in a fight [that] took place in Gulu village. I was shot on my neck and my fellow girls -- on seeing me -- ran and comforted me, telling me that God will help. We thought of nothing else but God.

These rebels would get civilian people, beat them to the point of death, then leave them suffering [and in] pain. Some they killed straight away. Young boys and girls of five and over were abducted.

One time, a girl who was abducted from a certain village tried to escape, but was caught by the rebels. The girl was brought in front of us and the rebels told us to stomp [her] to death. We killed the poor innocent girl, who thought of nothing but [trying to] rescue herself from them. If we did not kill the girl we were going to be shot by guns. We prayed for that girl in our hearts, silently, and asked God to pardon us and forgive us because it was not of our will to kill her. Six of our girls succeeded in escaping. The [remaining] twenty-four of us were taken to Sudan. We walked on foot up to Sudan. Before we had reached Sudan there was lack of water. Boys and girls died because of thirst on the way.

When we reached Kony's camp, we were in very bad [shape], and our feet were all flesh, with blood bleeding all through. Kony told us that we should never mind that, for those wounds will get cured, etc. But in our hearts we were not happy at all.

In Sudan, we worked just like slaves, cutting grass for thatching their huts, and also cutting grass for the Arabs when they demanded. We used to grind sorghum for bread, and our hands got sore because we were not used to such work.

Whenever the Ugandans announced over the radio that we [thirty girls should] be released, they would come and beat us, [asking] why [they were] always talking of us, who [were] we to be so important to the government, and maybe they will kill us. But we only prayed. I realized that the more we suffered, the more we became stronger in everything, especially in God.

Student letter #3

These rebels broke into our school on the ninth of October 1996. We traveled with them for long distances and among the rebels [there] were young boys who had been abducted from their homes. They have now become very used to being rebels. There were very young girls. Some [who had been there a long time] were women and men.

When we reached a certain mountain I took courage to ask one girl who was a rebel to tell us what made her become involved in such a thing. She told us that even she was abducted from her home, and it was not to her liking to be a rebel, but she was forced to. We asked why does she not try to escape when she gets a chance, like when they came to abduct us? She answered that they abducted her when she was still very young, and she has now given up hope of returning; she grew up in the hands of the rebels and she says she does not remember her home. When this girl told me this I began to weep and say to myself, look at this poor innocent girl who is really suffering, and I [am] now going to become like her! I felt that my life was already ruined, my education had come to an end, and I had now become an enemy to peace in Uganda.

I asked another boy who was friendly to us. I asked him why he had not escaped. The boy answered very briefly, because there were escorts near him-- all the abducted school boys were guarded, for the fear of their escape. He said that he was abducted from Sir Samuel Baker School in Gulu, he was going to sit for his final exams when the rebels abducted them. He said that the purpose of the abduction was that Joseph Kony had suggested that they should take us in order for some to become his soldiers and he also needed girls for his wives and the wives of people in rank.

On hearing this, I felt deeply hurt and prayed to God to help us, and especially help our leader, his Excellency the President, to find a solution to liberate us from this painful experience. The boy promised me that some girls would be released. Some who are unlucky ones would remain. He promised me that if I remained, he would try his best to escape with me.

Then, to my surprise, an army plane came and we were forced to go under the bushes. God helped me to escape when the plane was busy firing. Some time later, some of our girls who had managed to escape told us that the boy from Sir Samuel Baker School had [also] escaped.

I also know of a situation when the rebels went into my village on [date], at night. They went into everyone's home and [asked] them if they were going to vote for Museveni. If you admitted [that you were going to] vote for Museveni, you were killed.

The summary of this experience of mine is that Kony has killed a lot of people and has abducted very many young children, who still have their bright future ahead of them and who are the future builders of a nation. Therefore, I flash back with the question: In what ways, [what] steps are you going to take to see that our twenty-one remaining girls and the other innocent children are released?

Student letter #4

I briefly want to narrate the story [of] how we were abducted from school in October 1996. At night, I was deeply asleep when suddenly I was awakened by a terrible [sound of] breaking windows. The rebels forced their way through the window and came into the dormitory. One of them gave me a terrible blow on my head and I got up quickly from under the bed [where I was hiding]; they tied all our hands and made us start moving in single lines.

With God's help I managed to escape [while they marched]. After escaping I came back to school and slept out in the banana plantation [near the school]. In the morning I packed some of my belongings which the rebels hadn't looted and went back home to Kitgum.

On reaching home, I found that the same thing [had] happened to my village. People from my homeland were in the most difficult moment of life. Over 500 people could be killed in a day; cutting people's ears, mouths, legs, and arms, were too common. My family had already fled to town and our home in the village was totally burnt. The rebels had destroyed every thing. My father was stopped from working. The produce he got from farming was helping him pay our school fees. Now there is no possibility for me to continue my studies as there is now nowhere my father can get money from. Now in school I cannot concentrate on my studies. Every time I am recalling what happened; sometimes I become afraid and think that the rebels will come back again. I also keep thinking how my family is suffering with all these difficulties. I feel very bad when I think about our girls who are still missing, and suffering a lot in Sudan.

Therefore, I'm here pleading to you to find a way of stopping this rebel activity so that we children of Northern Uganda could also share in the peace that other children in the world are sharing in. I also beg you to find a way to bring back our girls who are still missing, and all the children taken away from their parents here in Northern Uganda, so that they may come back and live in peace together with their parents. We children of Northern Uganda need peace. I've not lived in peace since I was born. These rebel activities started when I was young and they are still going on. We need Peace.

Student letter #5

When this thing happened, we thought it was the end of our life. Our future was in total darkness and we never thought [we would meet] our dear ones again. On being released we started thinking about how our remaining girls were, about what kind of world we are living in, what kind of government this is, how the government looks [upon] this destruction. If we are really the children of Uganda in the North, what can the government do to stop this?

Please, as you have a willing heart to help, please do! Look ahead to bring us into a peaceful [country]. It is worst for the villagers who have no voice to say a word. They weep day and night. Please try to convince the two governments [of Uganda and Sudan] to [act] as friends and chase the rebels [out of] their countries so that they have nowhere to stay. In this way peace can be possible. Is this not so miserable? I ask for more help from you to bring peace and children's rights to our country. We want to have a voice in our country to develop it, not destroy it.

Student letter #6

My name is ---, a student of St. Mary's College Aboke, am sixteen years of age, and in form three this year. I am also the official head girl of the school at present.

First of all, I would like to tell you what these merciless rebels do to the people. A good example I saw when they worked in my village in Kitgum district. These rebels loot, burn houses, beat people, cut off peoples' ears, mouths, noses, arms, and legs and then they leave you to suffer. Or if they come to a home, they close all the family members into a house and set fire to it. Further, they plant landmines on roads, which will kill a great number of travelers.

My appeal is both to the rebels, headed by Joseph Kony, and to the government of Uganda, headed by his excellency, Yoweri Museveni. Would you advise Kony to open his eyes and stop doing harm to innocent people who know nothing about politics? Would you encourage the government of Uganda to provide good security to all places in the North? With honest soldiers who would not bring problems to the local people. In addition, the government should improve on better methods of transport in the North, since it's obvious that the rebels plant their mines mostly on [dirt] roads.

Make both the Ugandan government and the Sudanese government have a good relationship, through peace talks rather than through using force to bring peace. If you only succeed in bringing back the abducted children from Sudan, what difference does it makes if the rebels continue to abduct more people? I pray that you, as a body, work harder to find a way of restoring peace in our district, country and the entire world.

Student letter #7
My Feelings about Our Girls in the Bush and Other People

My feelings about our girls in the bush is that if you can organize and bring back our girls so that they may continue with their studies it would be wonderful, and we should ask God to help you in different ways to lead back our girls.

An example: for me, who comes from Kitgum district, I have seen the destruction [caused by] rebels in our district and it was the worst. They came to our place in the village and caught five of my brothers and one was killed on the spot. There is no peace in Kitgum district at all. If you saw the children who were killed and burnt, you would not [be able to] say anything at all. The schools in Kitgum district are really suffering from these rebels.

If you could struggle to help the northern part of Uganda it would be the most wonderful thing. In Uganda we shall never forget you in our day-to-day life because you have come to pull us out of this problem as Jesus did for our sins.

Last Friday, just as we were coming back to school for our second term, we came across the rebels and they shot at our vehicle. Nobody was killed, but the driver just turned the corner [and went] back to Kitgum. We stayed home for two days and I came to school on Monday. When we were on the way, we found the path they had crossed and [they had left] a letter [saying] they have come to Kitgum, and Gulu should rest for some few months, and then they will attack both Kitgum and Gulu district. [This is a reference to the recent shift in rebel operations from Gulu to Kitgum].

We ask you kindly: if you can struggle and bring back the girls in the bush, and stop the way the rebels are killing and burning people, we would not know what to say about the wonderful miracle you have made by the power of God. As for the three years St. Mary College has been suffering, we ask for help from you and your organization to send us some teaching materials, [to] encourage us to study and help the world in [the] future.

Student letter #8
My Feeling About the Abducted People

In 1996 when those of Kony came to St. Mary's College Aboke, I was in primary seven. We were preparing for our primary leaving examination. When we heard that those of Aboke had been taken away by those of Kony, I ran mad, and was not able to do anything. My [older] sister had been taken away. I tried to cry with different types of sound but it was too late. She is still in the bush. If I start to think about my brother who had been abducted from the school also, I feel like I want to hit myself with stones but it is impossible to do that.

Please! Please! Please! If you can bring back our brothers and sisters who are suffering in the bush I think it will be much better. I am here in school now but doing badly because I am thinking about my sister and brother who have been taken away from school [by the rebels]. If I go home from school and I see my parents and how sad they are, I myself start to cry. I have much more to tell you, but the more words I write, that is the more sad I become. Thank you.

Student letter #9
We Need Peace and Freedom

My experiences about this violence in Northern Uganda: this violence is being headed by Kony Joseph, a born native of the northern part of Uganda. This violence had brought so much interruption [of] life in this part of the country. It has brought about several questions by the people to the government, who couldn't answer the questions, and many problems too:

1. Increase in street children- children who have lost both parents and relatives and they have nowhere to go and end up being street children.
2. This violence has also destroyed childrens' morals. The children don't live in peace. They lack law from their parents, as parents may be killed when children are still young.
3. There is starvation and famine in Northern Uganda. This violence and slave trade are more or less the same, because the people who are to dig or carry out agriculture are taken away by rebels [and must work for them]. Others are killed, hence no farming is carried out, thus the population starves.
4. Loss of lives. Especially in villages in Gulu and Kitgum people are being killed, especially children and the people who are to help us live proper [lives] in the future [are] also being killed.
5. Reduced educational standards. This violence [has] very much affected our education [and] future life. Most schools, especially in villages, have been burnt away, some teachers killed and given to the pupils to eat after cooking. So it becomes very difficult; the people who are supposed to take up positions in future are being destroyed.
6. God's words and services have been abandoned. For example, that leader of the rebels, Joseph Kony, was one of the choir in the church before starting this disturbance. Now God's own people [are] being chosen to carry out his services and are being killed [by rebels].

My wishes are first to pray very hard to God Almighty to grant peaceful, healthy, and courageous life to the people who are trying with all their effort to help stop this violence in the north. I also wish this man and the members could be destroyed completely so that we can live in peace. . . . I pray to God almighty to change [Kony's] mind so that he may realize that he is doing what God doesn't desire, killing innocent people, which is against the Ten Commandments, which say "Don't Kill".

Student letter #10

I am a girl 15 years old. From my experience since I was ten years old, I have a lot to tell about these rebels. My village is in Kitgum, the most affected district from the north [as well as] Gulu. I am an Acholi girl and this is what I see with my own eyes when I go back home for holidays. This is what the rebels have done:

*   they burnt houses or whole villages
*   abduct young children from 8 years onwards
*   they killed people using the panga
*   they cut your mouth with a knife or lock it with a padlock
*   they destroyed people's crops and burnt them
*   they cut people's ears
*   they cut off your legs when they find you walking
*   they killed the headmaster of a school and cooked him and made the pupils eat him
*   they can pluck out your eyes
*   they cut people's hands off. My uncle was found hiding and he was cut to pieces so much that you cannot think he is a person anymore.

My village was completely destroyed and we stay in the town now. This kind of thing has been going on for over seven years. Now, [that I have been] taken myself, I came to know the nature of the rebels and how hard life is.

There are thousands of young children the rebels have taken from their parents [that are] suffering the same experience as our girls are suffering. There are many people without a place to sleep [or] anything to eat, but there is nothing being done for them. Many thousands of people die in the camps ["protected camps"] because of sorrow and anger.

I have failed to understand what the government has done to stop these things. I have failed to understand why innocent people like our girls and all the other captives should suffer so much.

Kony is an unlearned person, and ignorant. He kills in the name of the Holy Spirit. He said it's God who has sent him to do such things. His rebel group claims that he is the holiest. They said it was the spirit who talked to Kony [and told them to] come and get us. They claim that they want to overpower the government. They said Jesus once captured his disciples, so that is why they capture us to become their disciples.

So to anyone who [will] read this. My questions is: what can we say and do for the thousands and thousands of young people, our 21 girls who are still suffering in the bush with Kony Joseph, and the hundreds of people who die there day and night? My question remains to the one who reads this and meditates over it.

Student letter #11

Here are my feeling towards what happened in our school, the abduction of our girls by Lord Joseph Kony, the rebel leader. Although country-wide, people on hearing [of our abduction] were filled with pity, others were not-- or just pretended.

When our school closed for a while after the abduction, the majority of the students, including me, tried [to attend] various schools country-wide, but the life and the atmosphere in these schools was not conducive. We were nick-named by our fellow students as "Kony Rebels" and many teachers and school administrators suspected us [of being] HIV+, and wherever we were, we were afraid of identifying ourselves as students of St. Mary's College, Aboke, or else they would try to isolate us. Teachers in these schools asked us to be tested for venereal disease. We did not know why such was suspected of us. The more they call us these names, the more we are reminded of the bitter experience we had on that hateful day we live to remember in our lives; we got burned psychologically.

It was recently that we found out why we were being suspected as AIDS victims. It was following the abduction, when rumors spread that all the students of the school were raped by the rebels. I am kindly appealing to you, the members of Human Right Watch, that the information [that all the] students [were] raped was false. None of us [were] raped except two girls, and those who did it were killed by their commanders.

So please, I would be so grateful if you make it clear to the public that we are free from AIDS and they should not look at us as misfits in any community. We love them [the community] and we want their love too. I think my feeling can be evidenced by the number of girls you saw who returned from the bush and are still students of this school. It is because they did not get any love anywhere else. They tried. Except for here, at "home", our school-- St. Mary's College.

Student letter #12

I am a girl of sixteen. It was very rough because the rebels came and attacked us in the night. I [felt like] I wasn't a human because the way they treated us was like [we were] animals. Some of my friends were beaten seriously. This caused a trauma in my heart that still exists. When the rebels attacked us, I did feel that we children from the north [were] not cared for by the government.

Why can't we children be put aside and not be involved in political affairs? Many children are being killed and dying, all because some one wants to take over the government. I think that there will be almost no future generation, as most of the children are captured.

I would urge you to make the world know that children shouldn't be involved in political affairs. This is for the betterment of their spiritual, physical, and mental health. We can never have peace of mind when there is killing and fighting all the time. It makes the atmospheric air polluted and gives us evil memories, which [isn't] the way to improve a peaceful world

To end, I would say that you should help to see that every child gets her rights, all over the world. So many children are being rejected by their parents and the government never reacts about citizens having their rights abused. The rebels have done the worst things, which must be stopped as soon as possible, or else the meaning of life will be no more- only hatred, disunity, and grief will fill this nation.

U.N. Convention on the Rights of the Child

Convention on the Rights of the Child, G.A. res. 44/25, annex, 44 U.N. GAOR Sup p. (No. 49) at 167, U.N. Doc. A/44/49 (1989).

PREAMBLE

The States Parties to the present Convention,

Considering that, in accordance with the principles proclaimed in the Charter of the United Nations, recognition of the inherent dignity and of the equal and inalienable rights of all members of the human family is the foundation of freedom, justice and peace in the world,

Bearing in mind that the peoples of the United Nations have, in the Charter, reaffirmed their faith in fundamental human rights and in the dignity and worth of the human person, and have determined to promote social progress and better standards of life in larger freedom,

Recognizing that the United Nations has, in the Universal Declaration of Human Rights and in the International Covenants on Human Rights, proclaimed and agreed that everyone is entitled to all the rights and freedoms set forth therein, without distinction of any kind, such as race, colour, sex, language, religion, political or other opinion, national or social origin, property, birth or other status,

Recalling that, in the Universal Declaration of Human Rights, the United Nations has proclaimed that childhood is entitled to special care and assistance,

Convinced that the family, as the fundamental group of society and the natural environment for the growth and well-being of all its members and particularly children, should be afforded the necessary protection and assistance so that it can fully assume its responsibilities within the community,

Recognizing that the child, for the full and harmonious development of his or her personality, should grow up in a family environment, in an atmosphere of happiness, love and understanding,

Considering that the child should be fully prepared to live an individual life in society, and brought up in the spirit of the ideals proclaimed in the Charter of the

United Nations, and in particular in the spirit of peace, dignity, tolerance, freedom, equality and solidarity,

Bearing in mind that the need to extend particular care to the child has been stated in the Geneva Declaration of the Rights of the Child of 1924 and in the Declaration of the Rights of the Child adopted by the General Assembly on 20 November 1959 and recognized in the Universal Declaration of Human Rights, in the International Covenant on Civil and Political Rights (in particular in articles 23 and 24), in the International Covenant on Economic, Social and Cultural Rights (in particular in article 10) and in the statutes and relevant instruments of specialized agencies and international organizations concerned with the welfare of children, '

Bearing in mind that, as indicated in the Declaration of the Rights of the Child, "the child, by reason of his physical and mental immaturity, needs special safeguards and care, including appropriate legal protection, before as well as after birth",

Recalling the provisions of the Declaration on Social and Legal Principles relating to the Protection and Welfare of Children, with Special Reference to Foster Placement and Adoption Nationally and Internationally; the United Nations Standard Minimum Rules for the Administration of Juvenile Justice (The Beijing Rules) ; and the Declaration on the Protection of Women and Children in Emergency and Armed Conflict,

Recognizing that, in all countries in the world, there are children living in exceptionally difficult conditions, and that such children need special consideration,

Taking due account of the importance of the traditions and cultural values of each people for the protection and harmonious development of the child,

Recognizing the importance of international co-operation for improving the living conditions of children in every country, in particular in the developing countries,

Have agreed as follows:

PART I

Article 1

For the purposes of the present Convention, a child means every human being below the age of eighteen years unless under the law applicable to the child, majority is attained earlier.

Article 2

1. States Parties shall respect and ensure the rights set forth in the present Convention to each child within their jurisdiction without discrimination of any kind, irrespective of the child's or his or her parent's or legal guardian's race, colour, sex, language, religion, political or other opinion, national, ethnic or social origin, property, disability, birth or other status.

2. States Parties shall take all appropriate measures to ensure that the child is protected against all forms of discrimination or punishment on the basis of the status, activities, expressed opinions, or beliefs of the child's parents, legal guardians, or family members.

Article 3

1. In all actions concerning children, whether undertaken by public or private social welfare institutions, courts of law, administrative authorities or legislative bodies, the best interests of the child shall be a primary consideration.

2. States Parties undertake to ensure the child such protection and care as is necessary for his or her well-being, taking into account the rights and duties of his or her parents, legal guardians, or other individuals legally responsible for him or her, and, to this end, shall take all appropriate legislative and administrative measures.

3. States Parties shall ensure that the institutions, services and facilities responsible for the care or protection of children shall conform with the standards established by competent authorities, particularly in the areas of safety, health, in the number and suitability of their staff, as well as competent supervision.

Article 4

States Parties shall undertake all appropriate legislative, administrative, and other measures for the implementation of the rights recognized in the present Convention. With regard to economic, social and cultural rights, States Parties shall undertake such measures to the maximum extent of their available resources and, where needed, within the framework of international co-operation.

Article 5

States Parties shall respect the responsibilities, rights and duties of parents or, where applicable, the members of the extended family or community as provided for by local custom, legal guardians or other persons legally responsible for the child, to provide, in a manner consistent with the evolving capacities of the child, appropriate direction and guidance in the exercise by the child of the rights recognized in the present Convention.

Article 6

1. States Parties recognize that every child has the inherent right to life.

2. States Parties shall ensure to the maximum extent possible the survival and development of the child.

Article 7

1. The child shall be registered immediately after birth and shall have the right from birth to a name, the right to acquire a nationality and. as far as possible, the right to know and be cared for by his or her parents.

2. States Parties shall ensure the implementation of these rights in accordance with their national law and their obligations under the relevant international instruments in this field, in particular where the child would otherwise be stateless.

Article 8

1. States Parties undertake to respect the right of the child to preserve his or her identity, including nationality, name and family relations as recognized by law without unlawful interference.

2. Where a child is illegally deprived of some or all of the elements of his or her identity, States Parties shall provide appropriate assistance and protection, with a view to re-establishing speedily his or her identity.

Article 9

1. States Parties shall ensure that a child shall not be separated from his or her parents against their will, except when competent authorities subject to judicial review determine, in accordance with applicable law and procedures, that such separation is necessary for the best interests of the child. Such determination may be necessary in a particular case such as one involving abuse or neglect of the child by the parents, or one where the parents are living separately and a decision must be made as to the child's place of residence.

2. In any proceedings pursuant to paragraph 1 of the present article, all interested parties shall be given an opportunity to participate in the proceedings and make their views known.

3. States Parties shall respect the right of the child who is separated from one or both parents to maintain personal relations and direct contact with both parents on a regular basis, except if it is contrary to the child's best interests.

4. Where such separation results from any action initiated by a State Party, such as the detention, imprisonment, exile, deportation or death (including death arising from any cause while the person is in the custody of the State) of one or both parents or of the child, that State Party shall, upon request, provide the parents, the child or, if appropriate, another member of the family with the essential information concerning the whereabouts of the absent member(s) of the family unless the provision of the information would be detrimental to the well-being of the child. States Parties shall further ensure that the submission of such a request shall of itself entail no adverse consequences for the person(s) concerned.

Article 10

1. In accordance with the obligation of States Parties under article 9, paragraph 1, applications by a child or his or her parents to enter or leave a State Party for the purpose of family reunification shall be dealt with by States Parties in a positive, humane and expeditious manner. States Parties shall further ensure that the submission of such a request shall entail no adverse consequences for the applicants and for the members of their family.

2. A child whose parents reside in different States shall have the right to maintain on a regular basis, save in exceptional circumstances personal relations and direct contacts with both parents. Towards that end and in accordance with the obligation of States Parties under article 9, paragraph 1, States Parties shall respect the right of the child and his or her parents to leave any country, including their own, and to enter their own country. The right to leave any country shall be subject only to such restrictions as are prescribed by law and which are necessary to protect the national security, public order (ordre public), public health or morals or the rights and freedoms of others and are consistent with the other rights recognized in the present Convention.

Article 11

1. States Parties shall take measures to combat the illicit transfer and non-return of children abroad.

2. To this end, States Parties shall promote the conclusion of bilateral or multilateral agreements or accession to existing agreements.

Article 12

1. States Parties shall assure to the child who is capable of forming his or her own views the right to express those views freely in all matters affecting the child, the views of the child being given due weight in accordance with the age and maturity of the child.

2. For this purpose, the child shall in particular be provided the opportunity to be heard in any judicial and administrative proceedings affecting the child, either directly, or through a representative or an appropriate body, in a manner consistent with the procedural rules of national law.

Article 13

1. The child shall have the right to freedom of expression; this right shall include freedom to seek, receive and impart information and ideas of all kinds, regardless of frontiers, either orally, in writing or in print, in the form of art, or through any other media of the child's choice.

2. The exercise of this right may be subject to certain restrictions, but these shall only be such as are provided by law and are necessary:

(a) For respect of the rights or reputations of others; or

(b) For the protection of national security or of public order (ordre public), or of public health or morals.

Article 14

1. States Parties shall respect the right of the child to freedom of thought, conscience and religion.

2. States Parties shall respect the rights and duties of the parents and, when applicable, legal guardians, to provide direction to the child in the exercise of his or her right in a manner consistent with the evolving capacities of the child.

3. Freedom to manifest one's religion or beliefs may be subject only to such limitations as are prescribed by law and are necessary to protect public safety, order, health or morals, or the fundamental rights and freedoms of others.

Article 15

1. States Parties recognize the rights of the child to freedom of association and to freedom of peaceful assembly.

2. No restrictions may be placed on the exercise of these rights other than those imposed in conformity with the law and which are necessary in a democratic society in the interests of national security or public safety, public order (ordre

public), the protection of public health or morals or the protection of the rights and freedoms of others.

Article 16

1. No child shall be subjected to arbitrary or unlawful interference with his or her privacy, family, home or correspondence, nor to unlawful attacks on his or her honour and reputation.
2. The child has the right to the protection of the law against such interference or attacks.

Article 17

States Parties recognize the important function performed by the mass media and shall ensure that the child has access to information and material from a diversity of national and international sources, especially those aimed at the promotion of his or her social, spiritual and moral well-being and physical and mental health. To this end, States Parties shall:

(a) Encourage the mass media to disseminate information and material of social and cultural benefit to the child and in accordance with the spirit of article 29;

(b) Encourage international co-operation in the production, exchange and dissemination of such information and material from a diversity of cultural, national and international sources;

(c) Encourage the production and dissemination of children's books;

(d) Encourage the mass media to have particular regard to the linguistic needs of the child who belongs to a minority group or who is indigenous;

(e) Encourage the development of appropriate guidelines for the protection of the child from information and material injurious to his or her well-being, bearing in mind the provisions of articles 13 and 18.

Article 18

1. States Parties shall use their best efforts to ensure recognition of the principle that both parents have common responsibilities for the upbringing and development of the child. Parents or, as the case may be, legal guardians, have the primary responsibility for the upbringing and development of the child. The best interests of the child will be their basic concern.
2. For the purpose of guaranteeing and promoting the rights set forth in the present Convention, States Parties shall render appropriate assistance to parents and legal guardians in the performance of their child-rearing responsibilities and shall ensure the development of institutions, facilities and services for the care of children.

3. States Parties shall take all appropriate measures to ensure that children of working parents have the right to benefit from child-care services and facilities for which they are eligible.

Article 19

1. States Parties shall take all appropriate legislative, administrative, social and educational measures to protect the child from all forms of physical or mental violence, injury or abuse, neglect or negligent treatment, maltreatment or exploitation, including sexual abuse, while in the care of parent(s), legal guardian(s) or any other person who has the care of the child.

2. Such protective measures should, as appropriate, include effective procedures for the establishment of social programmes to provide necessary support for the child and for those who have the care of the child, as well as for other forms of prevention and for identification, reporting, referral, investigation, treatment and follow-up of instances of child maltreatment described heretofore, and, as appropriate, for judicial involvement.

Article 20

1. A child temporarily or permanently deprived of his or her family environment, or in whose own best interests cannot be allowed to remain in that environment, shall be entitled to special protection and assistance provided by the State.

2. States Parties shall in accordance with their national laws ensure alternative care for such a child.

3. Such care could include, inter alia, foster placement, kafalah of Islamic law, adoption or if necessary placement in suitable institutions for the care of children. When considering solutions, due regard shall be paid to the desirability of continuity in a child's upbringing and to the child's ethnic, religious, cultural and linguistic background.

Article 21

States Parties that recognize and/or permit the system of adoption shall ensure that the best interests of the child shall be the paramount consideration and they shall:
(a) Ensure that the adoption of a child is authorized only by competent authorities who determine, in accordance with applicable law and procedures and on the basis of all pertinent and reliable information, that the adoption is permissible in view of the child's status concerning parents, relatives and legal guardians and that, if required, the persons concerned have given their informed consent to the adoption on the basis of such counseling as may be necessary;

(b) Recognize that inter-country adoption may be considered as an alternative means of child's care, if the child cannot be placed in a foster or an adoptive family or cannot in any suitable manner be cared for in the child's country of origin;

(c) Ensure that the child concerned by inter-country adoption enjoys safeguards and standards equivalent to those existing in the case of national adoption;

(d) Take all appropriate measures to ensure that, in inter-country adoption, the placement does not result in improper financial gain for those involved in it;

(e) Promote, where appropriate, the objectives of the present article by concluding bilateral or multilateral arrangements or agreements, and endeavour, within this framework, to ensure that the placement of the child in another country is carried out by competent authorities or organs.

Article 22

1. States Parties shall take appropriate measures to ensure that a child who is seeking refugee status or who is considered a refugee in accordance with applicable international or domestic law and procedures shall, whether unaccompanied or accompanied by his or her parents or by any other person, receive appropriate protection and humanitarian assistance in the enjoyment of applicable rights set forth in the present Convention and in other international human rights or humanitarian instruments to which the said States are Parties.

2. For this purpose, States Parties shall provide, as they consider appropriate, co-operation in any efforts by the United Nations and other competent intergovernmental organizations or non-governmental organizations co-operating with the United Nations to protect and assist such a child and to trace the parents or other members of the family of any refugee child in order to obtain information necessary for reunification with his or her family. In cases where no parents or other members of the family can be found, the child shall be accorded the same protection as any other child permanently or temporarily deprived of his or her family environment for any reason , as set forth in the present Convention.

Article 23

1. States Parties recognize that a mentally or physically disabled child should enjoy a full and decent life, in conditions which ensure dignity, promote self-reliance and facilitate the child's active participation in the community.

2. States Parties recognize the right of the disabled child to special care and shall encourage and ensure the extension, subject to available resources, to the eligible child and those responsible for his or her care, of assistance for which application is made and which is appropriate to the child's condition and to the circumstances of the parents or others caring for the child.

3. Recognizing the special needs of a disabled child, assistance extended in accordance with paragraph 2 of the present article shall be provided free of charge, whenever possible, taking into account the financial resources of the parents or others caring for the child, and shall be designed to ensure that the disabled child has effective access to and receives education, training, health care services, rehabilitation services, preparation for employment and recreation opportunities in a manner conducive to the child's achieving the fullest possible social integration and individual development, including his or her cultural and spiritual development
4. States Parties shall promote, in the spirit of international cooperation, the exchange of appropriate information in the field of preventive health care and of medical, psychological and functional treatment of disabled children, including dissemination of and access to information concerning methods of rehabilitation, education and vocational services, with the aim of enabling States Parties to improve their capabilities and skills and to widen their experience in these areas. In this regard, particular account shall be taken of the needs of developing countries.

Article 24
1. States Parties recognize the right of the child to the enjoyment of the highest attainable standard of health and to facilities for the treatment of illness and rehabilitation of health. States Parties shall strive to ensure that no child is deprived of his or her right of access to such health care services.
2. States Parties shall pursue full implementation of this right and, in particular, shall take appropriate measures:
(a) To diminish infant and child mortality;
(b) To ensure the provision of necessary medical assistance and health care to all children with emphasis on the development of primary health care;
(c) To combat disease and malnutrition, including within the framework of primary health care, through, inter alia, the application of readily available technology and through the provision of adequate nutritious foods and clean drinking-water, taking into consideration the dangers and risks of environmental pollution;
(d) To ensure appropriate pre-natal and post-natal health care for mothers;
(e) To ensure that all segments of society, in particular parents and children, are informed, have access to education and are supported in the use of basic knowledge of child health and nutrition, the advantages of breastfeeding, hygiene and environmental sanitation and the prevention of accidents;
(f) To develop preventive health care, guidance for parents and family planning education and services.

3. States Parties shall take all effective and appropriate measures with a view to abolishing traditional practices prejudicial to the health of children.

4. States Parties undertake to promote and encourage international co-operation with a view to achieving progressively the full realization of the right recognized in the present article. In this regard, particular account shall be taken of the needs of developing countries.

Article 25

States Parties recognize the right of a child who has been placed by the competent authorities for the purposes of care, protection or treatment of his or her physical or mental health, to a periodic review of the treatment provided to the child and all other circumstances relevant to his or her placement.

Article 26

1. States Parties shall recognize for every child the right to benefit from social security, including social insurance, and shall take the necessary measures to achieve the full realization of this right in accordance with their national law.

2. The benefits should, where appropriate, be granted, taking into account the resources and the circumstances of the child and persons having responsibility for the maintenance of the child, as well as any other consideration relevant to an application for benefits made by or on behalf of the child.

Article 27

1. States Parties recognize the right of every child to a standard of living adequate for the child's physical, mental, spiritual, moral and social development.

2. The parent(s) or others responsible for the child have the primary responsibility to secure, within their abilities and financial capacities, the conditions of living necessary for the child's development.

3. States Parties, in accordance with national conditions and within their means, shall take appropriate measures to assist parents and others responsible for the child to implement this right and shall in case of need provide material assistance and support programmes, particularly with regard to nutrition, clothing and housing.

4. States Parties shall take all appropriate measures to secure the recovery of maintenance for the child from the parents or other persons having financial responsibility for the child, both within the State Party and from abroad. In particular, where the person having financial responsibility for the child lives in a State different from that of the child, States Parties shall promote the accession to international agreements or the conclusion of such agreements, as well as the making of other appropriate arrangements.

Article 28

1. States Parties recognize the right of the child to education, and with a view to achieving this right progressively and on the basis of equal opportunity, they shall, in particular:

(a) Make primary education compulsory and available free to all;

(b) Encourage the development of different forms of secondary education, including general and vocational education, make them available and accessible to every child, and take appropriate measures such as the introduction of free education and offering financial assistance in case of need;

(c) Make higher education accessible to all on the basis of capacity by every appropriate means;

(d) Make educational and vocational information and guidance available and accessible to all children;

(e) Take measures to encourage regular attendance at schools and the reduction of drop-out rates.

2. States Parties shall take all appropriate measures to ensure that school discipline is administered in a manner consistent with the child's human dignity and in conformity with the present Convention.

3. States Parties shall promote and encourage international cooperation in matters relating to education, in particular with a view to contributing to the elimination of ignorance and illiteracy throughout the world and facilitating access to scientific and technical knowledge and modern teaching methods. In this regard, particular account shall be taken of the needs of developing countries.

Article 29

1. States Parties agree that the education of the child shall be directed to:

(a) The development of the child's personality, talents and mental and physical abilities to their fullest potential;

(b) The development of respect for human rights and fundamental freedoms, and for the principles enshrined in the Charter of the United Nations;

(c) The development of respect for the child's parents, his or her own cultural identity, language and values, for the national values of the country in which the child is living, the country from which he or she may originate, and for civilizations different from his or her own;

(d) The preparation of the child for responsible life in a free society, in the spirit of understanding, peace, tolerance, equality of sexes, and friendship among all peoples, ethnic, national and religious groups and persons of indigenous origin;

(e) The development of respect for the natural environment.

2. No part of the present article or article 28 shall be construed so as to interfere with the liberty of individuals and bodies to establish and direct educational institutions, subject always to the observance of the principle set forth in paragraph 1 of the present article and to the requirements that the education given in such institutions shall conform to such minimum standards as may be laid down by the State.

Article 30
In those States in which ethnic, religious or linguistic minorities or persons of indigenous origin exist, a child belonging to such a minority or who is indigenous shall not be denied the right, in community with other members of his or her group, to enjoy his or her own culture, to profess and practice his or her own religion, or to use his or her own language.

Article 31
1. States Parties recognize the right of the child to rest and leisure, to engage in play and recreational activities appropriate to the age of the child and to participate freely in cultural life and the arts.
2. States Parties shall respect and promote the right of the child to participate fully in cultural and artistic life and shall encourage the provision of appropriate and equal opportunities for cultural, artistic, recreational and leisure activity.

Article 32
1. States Parties recognize the right of the child to be protected from economic exploitation and from performing any work that is likely to be hazardous or to interfere with the child's education, or to be harmful to the child's health or physical, mental, spiritual, moral or social development.
2. States Parties shall take legislative, administrative, social and educational measures to ensure the implementation of the present article. To this end, and having regard to the relevant provisions of other international instruments, States Parties shall in particular:
(a) Provide for a minimum age or minimum ages for admission to employment;
(b) Provide for appropriate regulation of the hours and conditions of employment;
(c) Provide for appropriate penalties or other sanctions to ensure the effective enforcement of the present article.

Article 33.
States Parties shall take all appropriate measures, including legislative, administrative, social and educational measures, to protect children from the illicit

use of narcotic drugs and psychotropic substances as defined in the relevant international treaties, and to prevent the use of children in the illicit production and trafficking of such substances.

Article 34

States Parties undertake to protect the child from all forms of sexual exploitation and sexual abuse. For these purposes, States Parties shall in particular take all appropriate national, bilateral and multilateral measures to prevent:
(a) The inducement or coercion of a child to engage in any unlawful sexual activity;
(b) The exploitative use of children in prostitution or other unlawful sexual practices;
(c) The exploitative use of children in pornographic performances and materials.

Article 35

States Parties shall take all appropriate national, bilateral and multilateral measures to prevent the abduction of, the sale of or traffic in children for any purpose or in any form.

Article 36

States Parties shall protect the child against all other forms of exploitation prejudicial to any aspects of the child's welfare.

Article 37

States Parties shall ensure that:
(a) No child shall be subjected to torture or other cruel, inhuman or degrading treatment or punishment. Neither capital punishment nor life imprisonment without possibility of release shall be imposed for offenses committed by persons below eighteen years of age;
(b) No child shall be deprived of his or her liberty unlawfully or arbitrarily. The arrest, detention or imprisonment of a child shall be in conformity with the law and shall be used only as a measure of last resort and for the shortest appropriate period of time;
(c) Every child deprived of liberty shall be treated with humanity and respect for the inherent dignity of the human person, and in a manner which takes into account the needs of persons of his or her age. In particular, every child deprived of liberty shall be separated from adults unless it is considered in the child's best interest not to do so and shall have the right to maintain contact with his or her family through correspondence and visits, save in exceptional circumstances;

(d) Every child deprived of his or her liberty shall have the right to prompt access to legal and other appropriate assistance, as well as the right to challenge the legality of the deprivation of his or her liberty before a court or other competent, independent and impartial authority, and to a prompt decision on any such action.

Article 38

1. States Parties undertake to respect and to ensure respect for rules of international humanitarian law applicable to them in armed conflicts which are relevant to the child.

2. States Parties shall take all feasible measures to ensure that persons who have not attained the age of fifteen years do not take a direct part in hostilities.

3. States Parties shall refrain from recruiting any person who has not attained the age of fifteen years into their armed forces. In recruiting among those persons who have attained the age of fifteen years but who have not attained the age of eighteen years, States Parties shall endeavor to give priority to those who are oldest.

4. In accordance with their obligations under international humanitarian law to protect the civilian population in armed conflicts, States Parties shall take all feasible measures to ensure protection and care of children who are affected by an armed conflict.

Article 39

States Parties shall take all appropriate measures to promote physical and psychological recovery and social reintegration of a child victim of: any form of neglect, exploitation, or abuse; torture or any other form of cruel, inhuman or degrading treatment or punishment; or armed conflicts. Such recovery and reintegration shall take place in an environment which fosters the health, self-respect and dignity of the child.

Article 40

1. States Parties recognize the right of every child alleged as, accused of, or recognized as having infringed the penal law to be treated in a manner consistent with the promotion of the child's sense of dignity and worth, which reinforces the child's respect for the human rights and fundamental freedoms of others and which takes into account the child's age and the desirability of promoting the child's reintegration and the child's assuming a constructive role in society.

2. To this end, and having regard to the relevant provisions of international instruments, States Parties shall, in particular, ensure that:

(a) No child shall be alleged as, be accused of, or recognized as having infringed the penal law by reason of acts or omissions that were not prohibited by national or international law at the time they were committed;

(b) Every child alleged as or accused of having infringed the penal law has at least the following guarantees:

(i) To be presumed innocent until proven guilty according to law;

(ii) To be informed promptly and directly of the charges against him or her, and, if appropriate, through his or her parents or legal guardians, and to have legal or other appropriate assistance in the preparation and presentation of his or her defense;

(iii) To have the matter determined without delay by a competent, independent and impartial authority or judicial body in a fair hearing according to law, in the presence of legal or other appropriate assistance and, unless it is considered not to be in the best interest of the child, in particular, taking into account his or her age or situation, his or her parents or legal guardians;

(iv) Not to be compelled to give testimony or to confess guilt; to examine or have examined adverse witnesses and to obtain the participation and examination of witnesses on his or her behalf under conditions of equality;

(v) If considered to have infringed the penal law, to have this decision and any measures imposed in consequence thereof reviewed by a higher competent, independent and impartial authority or judicial body according to law;

(vi) To have the free assistance of an interpreter if the child cannot understand or speak the language used;

(vii) To have his or her privacy fully respected at all stages of the proceedings. 3. States Parties shall seek to promote the establishment of laws, procedures, authorities and institutions specifically applicable to children alleged as, accused of, or recognized as having infringed the penal law, and, in particular:

(a) The establishment of a minimum age below which children shall be presumed not to have the capacity to infringe the penal law;

(b) Whenever appropriate and desirable, measures for dealing with such children without resorting to judicial proceedings, providing that human rights and legal safeguards are fully respected.

4. A variety of dispositions, such as care, guidance and supervision orders; counseling; probation; foster care; education and vocational training programmes and other alternatives to institutional care shall be available to ensure that children are dealt with in a manner appropriate to their well-being and proportionate both to their circumstances and the offense.

Article 41

Nothing in the present Convention shall affect any provisions which are more conducive to the realization of the rights of the child and which may be contained in:
(a) The law of a State party; or
(b) International law in force for that State.

PART II

Article 42

States Parties undertake to make the principles and provisions of the Convention widely known, by appropriate and active means, to adults and children alike.

Article 43

1. For the purpose of examining the progress made by States Parties in achieving the realization of the obligations undertaken in the present Convention, there shall be established a Committee on the Rights of the Child, which shall carry out the functions hereinafter provided.
2. The Committee shall consist of ten experts of high moral standing and recognized competence in the field covered by this Convention. The members of the Committee shall be elected by States Parties from among their nationals and shall serve in their personal capacity, consideration being given to equitable geographical distribution, as well as to the principal legal systems.
3. The members of the Committee shall be elected by secret ballot from a list of persons nominated by States Parties. Each State Party may nominate one person from among its own nationals.
4. The initial election to the Committee shall be held no later than six months after the date of the entry into force of the present Convention and thereafter every second year. At least four months before the date of each election, the Secretary-General of the United Nations shall address a letter to States Parties inviting them to submit their nominations within two months. The Secretary-General shall subsequently prepare a list in alphabetical order of all

persons thus nominated, indicating States Parties which have nominated them, and shall submit it to the States Parties to the present Convention.

5. The elections shall be held at meetings of States Parties convened by the Secretary-General at United Nations Headquarters. At those meetings, for which two thirds of States Parties shall constitute a quorum, the persons elected to the Committee shall be those who obtain the largest number of votes and an absolute majority of the votes of the representatives of States Parties present and voting.

6. The members of the Committee shall be elected for a term of four years. They shall be eligible for re-election if renominated. The term of five of the members elected at the first election shall expire at the end of two years; immediately after the first election, the names of these five members shall be chosen by lot by the Chairman of the meeting.

7. If a member of the Committee dies or resigns or declares that for any other cause he or she can no longer perform the duties of the Committee, the State Party which nominated the member shall appoint another expert from among its nationals to serve for the remainder of the term, subject to the approval of the Committee.

8. The Committee shall establish its own rules of procedure.

9. The Committee shall elect its officers for a period of two years.

10. The meetings of the Committee shall normally be held at United Nations Headquarters or at any other convenient place as determined by the Committee. The Committee shall normally meet annually. The duration of the meetings of the Committee shall be determined, and reviewed, if necessary, by a meeting of the States Parties to the present Convention, subject to the approval of the General Assembly.

11. The Secretary-General of the United Nations shall provide the necessary staff and facilities for the effective performance of the functions of the Committee under the present Convention.

12. With the approval of the General Assembly, the members of the Committee established under the present Convention shall receive emoluments from United Nations resources on such terms and conditions as the Assembly may decide.

Article 44

1. States Parties undertake to submit to the Committee, through the Secretary-General of the United Nations, reports on the measures they have adopted which give effect to the rights recognized herein and on the progress made on the enjoyment of those rights:

(a) Within two years of the entry into force of the Convention for the State Party concerned;

(b) Thereafter every five years.

2. Reports made under the present article shall indicate factors and difficulties, if any, affecting the degree of fulfilment of the obligations under the present Convention. Reports shall also contain sufficient information to provide the Committee with a comprehensive understanding of the implementation of the Convention in the country concerned.

3. A State Party which has submitted a comprehensive initial report to the Committee need not, in its subsequent reports submitted in accordance with paragraph 1 (b) of the present article, repeat basic information previously provided.

4. The Committee may request from States Parties further information relevant to the implementation of the Convention.

5. The Committee shall submit to the General Assembly, through the Economic and Social Council, every two years, reports on its activities.

6. States Parties shall make their reports widely available to the public in their own countries.

Article 45

In order to foster the effective implementation of the Convention and to encourage international co-operation in the field covered by the Convention:

(a) The specialized agencies, the United Nations Children's Fund, and other United Nations organs shall be entitled to be represented at the consideration of the implementation of such provisions of the present Convention as fall within the scope of their mandate. The Committee may invite the specialized agencies, the United Nations Children's Fund and other competent bodies as it may consider appropriate to provide expert advice on the implementation of the Convention in areas falling within the scope of their respective mandates. The Committee may invite the specialized agencies, the United Nations Children's Fund, and other United Nations organs to submit reports on the implementation of the Convention in areas falling within the scope of their activities;

(b) The Committee shall transmit, as it may consider appropriate, to the specialized agencies, the United Nations Children's Fund and other competent bodies, any reports from States Parties that contain a request, or indicate a need, for technical advice or assistance, along with the Committee's observations and suggestions, if any, on these requests or indications;

(c) The Committee may recommend to the General Assembly to request the Secretary-General to undertake on its behalf studies on specific issues relating to the rights of the child;

(d) The Committee may make suggestions and general recommendations based on information received pursuant to articles 44 and 45 of the present Convention. Such suggestions and general recommendations shall be transmitted to any State Party concerned and reported to the General Assembly, together with comments, if any, from States Parties.

PART III

Article 46
The present Convention shall be open for signature by all States.

Article 47
The present Convention is subject to ratification. Instruments of ratification shall be deposited with the Secretary-General of the United Nations.

Article 48
The present Convention shall remain open for accession by any State. The instruments of accession shall be deposited with the Secretary-General of the United Nations.

Article 49
1. The present Convention shall enter into force on the thirtieth day following the date of deposit with the Secretary-General of the United Nations of the twentieth instrument of ratification or accession.
2. For each State ratifying or acceding to the Convention after the deposit of the twentieth instrument of ratification or accession, the Convention shall enter into force on the thirtieth day after the deposit by such State of its instrument of ratification or accession.

Article 50
1. Any State Party may propose an amendment and file it with the Secretary-General of the United Nations. The Secretary-General shall thereupon communicate the proposed amendment to States Parties, with a request that they indicate whether they favor a conference of States Parties for the purpose of considering and voting upon the proposals. In the event that, within four months from the date of such communication, at least one third of the States Parties favor such a conference, the Secretary-General shall convene the conference under the auspices of the United Nations. Any amendment adopted by a majority of States Parties present and voting at the conference shall be submitted to the General Assembly for approval.

2. An amendment adopted in accordance with paragraph 1 of the present article shall enter into force when it has been approved by the General Assembly of the United Nations and accepted by a two-thirds majority of States Parties.

3. When an amendment enters into force, it shall be binding on those States Parties which have accepted it, other States Parties still being bound by the provisions of the present Convention and any earlier amendments which they have accepted.

Article 51

1. The Secretary-General of the United Nations shall receive and circulate to all States the text of reservations made by States at the time of ratification or accession.

2. A reservation incompatible with the object and purpose of the present Convention shall not be permitted.

3. Reservations may be withdrawn at any time by notification to that effect addressed to the Secretary-General of the United Nations, who shall then inform all States. Such notification shall take effect on the date on which it is received by the Secretary-General

Article 52

A State Party may denounce the present Convention by written notification to the Secretary-General of the United Nations. Denunciation becomes effective one year after the date of receipt of the notification by the Secretary-General.

Article 53

The Secretary-General of the United Nations is designated as the depositary of the present Convention.

Article 54

The original of the present Convention, of which the Arabic, Chinese, English, French, Russian and Spanish texts are equally authentic, shall be deposited with the Secretary-General of the United Nations.

IN WITNESS THEREOF the undersigned plenipotentiaries, being duly authorized thereto by their respective governments, have signed the present Convention.

APPENDIX C
African Charter on the Rights and Welfare of the Child[113]
OAU Doc. CAB/LEG/24.9/49 (1990).

PREAMBLE

The African Member States of the Organization of African Unity, Parties to the present Charter entitled "African Charter on the Rights and Welfare of the Child",

Considering that the Charter of the Organization of African Unity recognizes the paramountcy of Human Rights and the African Charter on Human and People's Rights proclaimed and agreed that everyone is entitled to all the rights and freedoms recognized and guaranteed therein, without distinction of any kind such as race, ethnic group, colour, sex, language, religion, political or any other opinion, national and social origin, fortune, birth or other status;

Recalling the Declaration on the Rights and welfare of the African Child (AHG/ST.4 Rev.I) adopted by the Assembly of Heads of State and Government of the Organization of African Unity, at its Sixteenth Ordinary Session in Monrovia, Liberia from 17 to 20 July 1979, recognized the need to take all appropriate measures to promote and protect the rights and welfare of the African Child;

Noting with concern that the situation of most African children, remains critical due to the unique factors of their socioeconomic, cultural, traditional and developmental circumstances, natural disasters, armed conflicts, exploitation and hunger, and on account of the child's physical and mental immaturity he/she needs special safeguards and care;

Recognizing that the child occupies a unique and privileged position in the African society and that for the full and harmonious development of his personality. the child should grow up in a family environment in an atmosphere of happiness, love and understanding;

---

[113] As of the date of publication of this report, the African Charter on the Rights and Welfare of the Child had not yet entered into force.

Recognizing that the child, due to the needs of his physical and mental development requires particular care with regard to health, physical, mental, moral and social development, and requires legal protection in conditions of freedom, dignity and security;

Taking into consideration the virtues of their cultural heritage, historical background and the values of the African civilization which should inspire and characterize their reflection on the concept of the rights and welfare of the child;

Considering that the promotion and protection of the rights and welfare of the child also implies the performance of duties on the part of everyone;

Reaffirming adherence to the principles of the rights and welfare of the child contained in the declaration, conventions and other instruments of the Organization of African Unity and in the United Nations and in particular the United Nations Convention on the Rights of the Child; and the OAU Heads of State and Government's Declaration on the Rights and Welfare of the African Child.

HAVE AGREED AS FOLLOWS:

PART 1: RIGHTS AND DUTIES

CHAPTER ONE: RIGHTS AND WELFARE OF THE CHILD

Article 1: Obligation of States Parties
1. The Member States of the Organization of African Unity Parties to the present Charter shall recognize the rights, freedoms and duties enshrined in this Charter and shall undertake to take the necessary steps, in accordance with their Constitutional processes and with the provisions of the present Charter, to adopt such legislative or other measures as may be necessary to give effect to the provisions of this Charter.
2. Nothing in this Charter shall affect any provisions that are more conductive to the realization of the rights and welfare of the child contained in the law of a State Party or in any other international convention or agreement in force in that State.
3. Any custom, tradition, cultural or religious practice that is inconsistent with the rights, duties and obligations contained in the present Charter shall to the extent of such inconsistency be discouraged.

Article 2: Definition of a Child
For the purposes of this Charter. a child means every human being below the age of 18 years.

Article 3: Non-Discrimination
Every child shall be entitled to the enjoyment of the rights and freedoms recognized and guaranteed in this Charter irrespective of the child's or his/her parents' or legal guardians' race, ethnic group, colour, sex, language, religion, political or other opinion, national and social origin, fortune, birth or other status.

Article 4: Best Interests of the Child
1. In all actions concerning the child undertaken by any person or authority the best interests of the child shall be the primary consideration.
2. In all judicial or administrative proceedings affecting a child who is capable of communicating his/her own views, and opportunity shall be provided for the views of the child to be heard either directly or through an impartial representative as a party to the proceedings and those views shall be taken into consideration by the relevant authority in accordance with the provisions of appropriate law.

Article 5: Survival and Development
1. Every child has an inherent right to life. This right shall be protected by law.
2. States Parties to the present Charter shall ensure, to the maximum extent possible, the survival, protection and development of the child.
3. Death sentence shall not be pronounced for crimes committed by children.

Article 6: Name and Nationality
1. Every child shall have the right from his birth to a name.
2. Every child shall be registered immediately after birth.
3. Every child has the right to acquire a nationality.
4. States Parties to the present Charter shall undertake to ensure that their Constitutional legislation recognize the principles according to which a child shall acquire the nationality of the State in the territory of which he has been born if, at the time of the child's birth. he is not granted nationality by any other State in accordance with its laws.

Article 7: Freedom of Expression
Every child who is capable of communicating his or her own views shall be assured the rights to express his opinions freely in all matters and to disseminate his opinions subject to such restrictions as are prescribed by laws.

Article 8: Freedom of Association
Every child shall have the right to free association and freedom of peaceful assembly in conformity with the law.

Article 9: Freedom of Thought, Conscience and Religion
1. Every child shall have the right to freedom of thought conscience and religion.
2. Parents, and where applicable, legal guardians shall have a duty to provide guidance and direction in the exercise of these rights having regard to the evolving capacities, and best interests of the child.
3. States Parties shall respect the duty of parents and where applicable, legal guardians to provide guidance and direction in the enjoyment of these rights subject to the national laws and policies.

Article 10: Protection of Privacy
No child shall be subject to arbitrary or unlawful interference with his privacy, family, home or correspondence, or to the attacks upon his honour or reputation, provided that parents or legal guardians shall have the right to exercise reasonable supervision over the conduct of their children. The child has the right to the protection of the law against such interference or attacks.

Article 11: Education
1. Every child shall have the right to education.
2. The education of the child shall be directed to:

> (a) the promotion and development of the child's personality, talents and mental and physical abilities to their fullest potential;
> (b) fostering respect for human rights and fundamental freedoms with particular reference to those set out in the provisions of various African instruments on human and peoples' rights and international human rights declarations and conventions;
> (c) the preservation and strengthening of positive African morals, traditional values and cultures;
> (d) the preparation of the child for responsible life in a free society, in the spirit of understanding, tolerance, dialogue, mutual respect and friendship among all peoples ethnic, tribal and religious groups;
> (e) the preservation of national independence and territorial integrity;

(f) the promotion and achievements of African Unity and
solidarity;
(g) the development of respect for the environment and natural
resources;
(h) the promotion of the child's understanding of primary health
care.

3. States Parties to the present Charter shall take all appropriate measures with a
view to achieving the full realization of this right and shall in particular:

(a) provide free and compulsory basic education:
(b) encourage the development of secondary education in its
different forms and to progressively make it free and accessible
to all;
(c) make the higher education accessible to all on the basis of
capacity and ability by every appropriate means;
(d) take measures to encourage regular attendance at schools and
the reduction of drop-out rate;
(e) take special measures in respect of female, gifted and
disadvantaged children, to ensure equal access to education for
all sections of the community.

4. States Parties to the present Charter shall respect the rights and duties of parents,
and where applicable, of legal guardians to choose for their children's schools,
other than those established by public authorities, which conform to such minimum
standards may be approved by the State, to ensure the religious and moral
education of the child in a manner with the evolving capacities of the child.
5. States Parties to the present Charter shall take all appropriate measures to ensure
that a child who is subjected to school or parental discipline shall be treated with
humanity and with respect for the inherent dignity of the child and in conformity
with the present Charter.
6. States Parties to the present Charter shall have all appropriate measures to ensure
that children who become pregnant before completing their education shall have
an opportunity to continue with their education on the basis of their individual
ability.
7. No part of this Article shall be construed as to interfere with the liberty of
individuals and bodies to establish and direct educational institutions subject to the
observance of the principles set out in paragraph 1 of this Article and the

requirement that the education given in such institutions shall conform to such minimum standards as may be laid down by the State.

Article 12: Leisure, Recreation and Cultural Activities

1. States Parties recognize the right of the child to rest and leisure, to engage in play and recreational activities appropriate to the age of the child and to participate freely in cultural life and the arts.
2. States Parties shall respect and promote the right of the child to fully participate in cultural and artistic life and shall encourage the provision of appropriate and equal opportunities for cultural, artistic, recreational and leisure activity.

Article 13: Handicapped Children

1. Every child who is mentally or physically disabled shall have the right to special measures of protection in keeping with his physical and moral needs and under conditions which ensure his dignity, promote his self-reliance and active participation in the community.
2. States Parties to the present Charter shall ensure, subject to available resources, to a disabled child and to those responsible for his care, of assistance for which application is made and which is appropriate to the child's condition and in particular shall ensure that the disabled child has effective access to training, preparation for employment and recreation opportunities in a manner conducive to the child achieving the fullest possible social integration, individual development and his cultural and moral development.
3. The States Parties to the present Charter shall use their available resources with a view to achieving progressively the full convenience of the mentally and physically disabled person to movement and access to public highway buildings and other places to which the disabled may legitimately want to have access to.

Article 14: Health and Health Services

1. Every child shall have the right to enjoy the best attainable state of physical, mental and spiritual health.
2. States Parties to the present Charter shall undertake to pursue the full implementation of this right and in particular shall take measures:

    (a) to reduce infant and child moratality rate;
    (b) to ensure the provision of necessary medical assistance and
    health care to all children with emphasis on the development of
    primary health care;

(c) to ensure the provision of adequate nutrition and safe drinking water;

(d) to combat disease and malnutrition within the framework of primary health care through the application of appropriate technology;

(e) to ensure appropriate health care for expectant and nursing mothers;

(f) to develop preventive health care and family life education and provision of service;

(g) to integrate basic health service programme in national development plans;

(h) to ensure that all sectors of the society, in particular, parents, children, community leaders and community workers are informed and supported in the use of basic knowledge of child health and nutrition, the advantages of breast-feeding, hygiene and environmental sanitation and the prevention of domestic and other accidents;

(i) to ensure the meaningful participation of non-governmental organizations, local communities and the beneficiary population in the planning and management of a basic service programmes for children;

(j) to support through technical and financial means, the mobilization of local community resources in the development of primary health care for children.

Article 15: Child Labor

1. Every child shall be protected from all forms of economic exploitation and from performing any work that is likely to be hazardous or to interfere with the child's physical, mental, spiritual, moral, or social development.

2. States Parties to the present Charter take all appropriate legislative and administrative measures to ensure the full implementation of this Article which covers both the formal and informal sectors of employment and having regard to the relevant provisions of the International Labor Organization's instruments relating to children, States Parties shall in particular:

(a) provide through legislation, minimum wages for admission to every employment;

(b) provide for appropriate regulation of hours and conditions of employment;

(c) provide for appropriate penalties or other sanctions to ensure the effective enforcement of this Article;
(d) promote the dissemination of information on the hazards of child labour to all sectors of the community.

Article 16: Protection Against Child Abuse and Torture

1. States Parties to the present Charter shall take specific legislative, administrative, social and educational measures to protect the child from all forms of torture, inhuman or degrading treatment and especially physical or mental injury or abuse, neglect or maltreatment including sexual abuse, while in the care of a parent, legal guardian or school authority or any other person who has the care of the child.
2. Protective measures under this Article shall include effective procedures for the establishment of special monitoring units to provide necessary support for the child and for those who have the care of the child, as well as other forms of prevention and for identification, reporting, referral, investigation, treatment, and follow-up of instances of child abuse and neglect.

Article 17: Administration of Juvenile Justice

1. Every child accused or found guilty of having infringed penal law shall have the right to special treatment in a manner consistent with the child's sense of dignity and worth and which reinforces the child's respect for human rights and fundamental freedoms of others.
2. States Parties to the present Charter shall in particular:

(a) ensure that no child who is detained or imprisoned or otherwise deprived of his/her liberty is subjected to torture, inhuman or degrading treatment or punishment;
(b) ensure that children are separated from adults in their place of detention or imprisonment;
(c) ensure that every child accused in infringing the penal law:
(i) shall be presumed innocent until duly recognized guilty;
(ii) shall be informed promptly in a language that he understands and in detail of the charge against him, and shall be entitled to the assistance of an interpreter if he or she cannot understand the language used;
(iii) shall be afforded legal and other appropriate assistance in the preparation and presentation of his defense;

(iv) shall have the matter determined as speedily as possible by an impartial tribunal and if found guilty, be entitled to an appeal by a higher tribunal;

(v) shall not be compelled to give testimony or confess guilt.

(d) prohibit the press and the public from trial.

3. The essential aim of treatment of every child during the trial and also if found guilty of infringing the penal law shall be his or her reformation, re-integration into his or her family and social rehabilitation.

4. There shall be a minimum age below which children shall be presumed not to have the capacity to infringe the penal law.

Article 18: Protection of the Family

1. The family shall be the natural unit and basis of society. It shall enjoy the protection and support of the State for its establishment and development.

2. States Parties to the present Charter shall take appropriate steps to ensure equality of rights and responsibilities of spouses with regard to children during marriage and in the even of its dissolution. In case of the dissolution, provision shall be made for the necessary protection of the child.

3. No child shall be deprived of maintenance by reference to the parents' marital status.

Article 19: Parent Care and Protection

1. Every child shall be entitled to the enjoyment of parental care and protection and shall, whenever possible, have the right to reside with his or her parents. No child shall be separated from his parents against his will, except when a judicial authority determines in accordance with the appropriate law, that such separation is in the best interest of the child.

2. Every child who is separated from one or both parents shall have the right to maintain personal relations and direct contact with both parents on a regular basis.

3. Where separation results from the action of a State Party, the State Party shall provide the child, or if appropriate, another member of the family with essential information concerning the whereabouts of the absent member or members of the family. States Parties shall also ensure that the submission of such a request shall not entail any adverse consequences for the person or persons in whose respect it is made.

4. Where a child is apprehended by a State Party, his parents or guardians shall, as soon as possible, be notified of such apprehension by that State Party.

Article 20: Parental Responsibilities

1. Parents or other persons responsible for the child shall have the primary responsibility of the upbringing and development the child and shall have the duty:

> (a) to ensure that the best interests of the child are their basic concern at all times;
> (b) to secure, within their abilities and financial capacities, conditions of living necessary to the child's development; and
> (c) to ensure that domestic discipline is administered with humanity and in a manner consistent with the inherent dignity of the child.

2. States Parties to the present Charter shall in accordance with their means and national conditions the all appropriate measures;

> (a) to assist parents and other persons responsible for the child and in case of need provide material assistance and support programmes: particularly with regard to nutrition, health, education, clothing and housing;
> (b) to assist parents and others responsible for the child in the performance of child-rearing and ensure the development of institutions responsible for providing care of children; and
> (c) to ensure that the children of working parents are provided with care services and facilities.

Article 21: Protection against Harmful Social and Cultural Practices

1. States Parties to the present Charter shall take all appropriate measures to eliminate harmful social and cultural practices affecting the welfare, dignity, normal growth and development of the child and in particular:

> (a) those customs and practices prejudicial to the health or life of the child; and
> (b) those customs and practices discriminatory to the child on the grounds of sex or other status.

2. Child marriage and the betrothal of girls and boys shall be prohibited and effective action, including legislation, shall be taken to specify the minimum age of marriage to be 18 years and make registration of all marriages in an official registry compulsory.

Article 22: Armed Conflicts

1. States Parties to this Charter shall undertake to respect and ensure respect for rules of international humanitarian law applicable in armed conflicts which affect the child.

2. States Parties to the present Charter shall take all necessary measures to ensure that no child shall take a direct part in hostilities and refrain in particular, from recruiting any child.

3. States Parties to the present Charter shall, in accordance with their obligations under international law, protect the civilian population in armed conflicts and shall take all feasible measures to ensure the protection and care of children who are affected by armed conflicts. Such rules shall also apply to children in situations of internal armed conflicts, tension and strife.

Article 23: Refugee Children

1. States Parties to the present Charter shall take all appropriate measures to ensure that a child who is seeking refugee status or who is considered a refugee in accordance with applicable international or domestic law shall, whether unaccompanied or accompanied by parents, legal guardians or close relatives, receive appropriate protection and humanitarian assistance in the enjoyment of the rights set out in this Charter and other international human rights and humanitarian instruments to which the States are Parties.

2. States Parties shall undertake to co-operate with existing international organizations which protect and assist refugees in their efforts to protect and assist such a child and to trace the parents or other close relatives or an unaccompanied refugee child in order to obtain information necessary for reunification with the family.

3. Where no parents, legal guardians or close relatives can be found, the child shall be accorded the same protection as any other child permanently or temporarily deprived of his family environment for any reason.

4. The provisions of this Article apply *mutatis mutandis* to internally displaced children whether through natural disaster, internal armed conflicts, civil strife, breakdown of economic and social order or howsoever caused.

Article 24: Adoption

States Parties which recognize the system of adoption shall ensure that the best interest of the child shall be the paramount consideration and they shall:

(a) establish competent authorities to determine matters of adoption and carry out in accordance with applicable laws and procedures and on the basis of all relevant and reliable information. that the adoption is permissible in view of the child's status concerning parents, relatives and guardians and that, if necessary, the appropriate persons concerned have given their informed consent to the adoption on the basis of such counselling as may be necessary;

(b) recognize that inter-country adoption in those States who have ratified or adhered to the International Convention on the Rights of the Child or this Charter, may, as the last resort, be considered as an alternative means of a child's care, if the child cannot be placed in a foster or an adoptive family or cannot in any suitable manner be cared for in the child's country of origin;

(c) ensure that the child affected by inter-country adoption enjoys safeguards and standards equivalent to those existing in the case of national adoption;

(d) take all appropriate measures to ensure that in inter-country adoption, the placement does not result in trafficking or improper financial gain for those involved in it;

(e) promote, where appropriate, the objectives of this Article by concluding bilateral or multilateral arrangements or agreements, and endeavour, within this framework to ensure that the placement of the child in another country is carried out by competent authorities or organs;

(f) establish a machinery to monitor the well-being of the adopted child.

Article 25: Separation from Parents

1. Any child who is permanently or temporarily deprived of his family environment for any reason shall be entitled to special protection and assistance;
2. States Parties to the present Charter:

(a) shall ensure that a child who is parentless, or who is temporarily or permanently deprived of his or her family environment, or who in his or her best interest cannot be brought up or allowed to remain in that environment shall be provided with alternative family care, which could include, among others, foster placement, or placement in suitable institutions for the care of children;

(b) shall take all necessary measures to trace and re-unite children with parents or relatives where separation is caused by internal and external displacement arising from armed conflicts or natural disasters.

3. When considering alternative family care of the child and the best interests of the child, due regard shall be paid to the desirability of continuity in a child's up-bringing and to the child's ethnic, religious or linguistic background.

Article 26: Protection Against Apartheid and Discrimination

1. States Parties to the present Charter shall individually and collectively undertake to accord the highest priority to the special needs of children living under *Apartheid* and in States subject to military destabilization by the *Apartheid* regime.
2. States Parties to the present Charter shall individually and collectively undertake to accord the highest priority to the special needs of children living under regimes practicing racial, ethnic, religious or other forms of discrimination as well as in States subject to military destabilization.
3. States Parties shall undertake to provide whenever possible, material assistance to such children and to direct their efforts towards the elimination of all forms of discrimination and *Apartheid* on the African Continent.

Article 27: Sexual Exploitation

1. States Parties to the present Charter shall undertake to protect the child from all forms of sexual exploitation and sexual abuse and shall in particular take measures to prevent:

(a) the inducement, coercion or encouragement of a child to engage in any sexual activity;
(b) the use of children in prostitution or other sexual practices;
(c) the use of children in pornographic activities, performances and materials.

Article 28: Drug Abuse

States Parties to the present Charter shall take all appropriate measures to protect the child from the use of narcotics and illicit use of psychotropic substances as defined in the relevant international treaties, and to prevent the use of children in the production and trafficking of such substances.

Article 29: Sale, Trafficking and Abduction

States Parties to the present Charter shall take appropriate measures to prevent:

(a) the abduction, the sale of, or traffic in children for any purpose or in any form, by any person including parents or legal guardians of the child;

(b) the use of children in all forms of begging.

Article 30: Children of Imprisoned Mothers

1. States Parties to the present Charter shall undertake to provide special treatment to expectant mothers and to mothers of infants and young children who have been accused or found guilty of infringing the penal law and shall in particular:

(a) ensure that a non-custodial sentence will always be first considered when sentencing such mothers;

(b) establish and promote measures alternative to institutional confinement for the treatment of such mothers;

(c) establish special alternative institutions for holding such mothers;

(d) ensure that a mother shall not be imprisoned with her child;

(e) ensure that a death sentence shall not be imposed on such mothers;

(f) the essential aim of the penitentiary system will be the reformation, the integration of the mother to the family and social rehabilitation.

Article 31: Responsibilities of the Child

Every child shall have responsibilities towards his family and society, the State and other legally recognized communities and the international community. The child, subject to his age and ability, and such limitations as may be contained in the present Charter, shall have the duty;

(a) to work for the cohesion of the family, to respect his parents and elders at all times ro assist them in case of need;

(b) to serve his national community by placing his physical and intellectual abilities at its service;

(c) to preserve and strengthen social and national solidarity;

(d) to and strengthen African cultural values in his relations with other members of the society, in the spirit of tolerance, dialogue

and consultation and to contribute to the moral well-being of
society;
(e) to preserve and strengthen the independence and the integrity
of his country;
(f) to contribute to the best of his abilities, at all times and at all
levels, to the promotion and achievement of African Unity.

Draft Optional Protocol to the Convention on
the Rights of the Child on Involvement of Children in Armed Conflicts[114]

The States Parties to the present Protocol,

Encouraged by the overwhelming support for the Convention on the Rights of the Child, demonstrating the widespread commitment that exists to strive for the promotion and protection of the rights of the child,

Reaffirming that the rights of children require special protection and call for continuous improvement of the situation of children without distinction, as well as for their development and education in conditions of peace and security,

---

[114] In 1994, the U.N. Commission on Human Rights decided to establish an open-ended inter-sessional working group to elaborate a draft optional protocol to the Convention on the Rights of the Child on the involvement of children in armed conflicts. Article 38 of the Convention on the Rights of the Child sets fifteen years as the minimum age for recruitment and participation in hostilities. The purpose of the draft optional protocol is to raise that age. Sessions of the working group were held in the autumn of 1994, January 1996, and January 1997.

This is the text of the draft optional protocol as it emerged from the third session of the working group in January 1997. The fourth session of the working group will take place in January 1998. Once finalized, the draft text will be submitted to the U.N. Commission on Human Rights, and ultimately to the U.N. General Assembly. The optional protocol will be opened for signature by any State which is a signatory to the Convention on the Rights of the Child. The optional protocol will be subject to ratification or open to accession by any State which has ratified or acceded to the Convention.

Bracketed language is language that has not yet been agreed upon by members of the working group. Note that the working group has agreed to set the age for compulsory recruitment into government armed forces at eighteen (Draft Article 2). Disagreement exists on the minimum age for voluntary recruitment into government armed forces (Draft Article 3), and for participation in hostilities (Draft Article 1).

It should be noted that the U.S. government has played a key role in preventing the working group from reaching an agreement on the minimum age for participation in hostilities (Draft Article 1). At the last session of the working group, the U.S. government stated that it would refuse to accept eighteen as the minimum age; all other governments participating in the working group supported, or were willing to support, eighteen as the minimum age.

Considering that to further strengthen the implementation of rights recognized in the Convention on the Rights of the Child, there is a need to increase the protection of children from involvement in armed conflicts,

Noting that Article 1 of the Convention on the Rights of the Child specifies that, for the purpose of that Convention, a child means every human being below the age of 18 years unless under the law applicable to the child, majority is attained earlier,

Convinced that an Optional Protocol to the Convention, raising the age of possible recruitment of persons into armed forces and their participation in hostilities, will contribute effectively to the implementation of the principle that the best interests of the child are to be a primary consideration in all actions concerning children,

Noting with satisfaction that the twenty-sixth International Conference of the Red Cross and Red Crescent in December 1995 recommended that parties to conflict take every feasible step to ensure that children under the age of 18 years do not take part in hostilities,

Bearing in mind that conditions of peace and security based on full respect of the purposes and principles contained in the Charter of the United Nations and observance of applicable human rights instruments are indispensable for the full protection of children, in particular during armed conflicts and foreign occupation,

Convinced of the need to strengthen international cooperation regarding the physical and psychosocial rehabilitation and social reintegration of children who are victims of armed conflicts,

Recognizing with grave concern the growing trend towards recruitment, training and use of children in hostilities by armed groups,

Have agreed as follows:

Article 1
States Parties shall take all feasible measures to ensure that persons who have not attained the age of [18][17] years do not take [a direct] part in hostilities.

Article 2

1. States Parties shall ensure that persons who have not attained the age of 18 years are not compulsorily recruited into their armed forces.

2. States Parties shall ensure that persons who have not attained the age of [16] [17] [18] years are not voluntarily recruited into their armed forces.

3. States Parties shall ensure that every person who chooses to enlist into their armed forces before reaching the age of 18 does so of his or her own free will and, unless he or she has already attained majority, with the full and informed consent of those legally responsible for him or her.

4. [Paragraph 2 does not apply to education and vocational training in establishments operated by or under the control of the armed forces of the States Parties in keeping with articles 28 and 29 of the Convention on the Rights of the Child]

New article A

[States Parties shall take all appropriate measures to prevent recruitment of persons under the age of 18 years by non-governmental armed groups involved in hostilities.]

Article 3

Nothing in the present Protocol shall be construed so as to preclude provisions in the law of a State Party or in international instruments and international humanitarian law which are more conducive to the realization of the rights of the child.

Article 4

[No reservation is admissible to the present Protocol.]
OR
[No reservation is admissible to articles ... and ... of the present Protocol.]
OR
[A reservation incompatible with the object and the purpose of the present Protocol shall not be permitted.]

Article 5

The States Parties to the present Protocol shall include in the reports they submit to the Committee on the Rights of the Child, in accordance with article 44 of the Convention, information on the measures that they have adopted to give effect to the present Protocol.

New article D

[1. If the Committee receives reliable information which appears to it to contain well-founded indications that recruitment or use of children in hostilities, contrary to the provisions of the present Protocol, is being
practiced in the territory of a State Party, the Committee may request the observations of the State Party with regard to the information concerned.

2. Taking into account any observations which may have been submitted by the State Party concerned, as well as any other relevant information available to it, the Committee may:

    (a) Seek further clarification, information or comments from any source,
    including where applicable the source(s) of the original information;
    (b) Hold hearings in order to clarify the situation.

3. The Committee may initiate a confidential inquiry, which may include a visit of its members (2-3) to the territory of the State Party concerned:

    (a) Such a visit could take place only with the consent/after the consultation with the State Party concerned;
    (b) If an inquiry is made in accordance with the present paragraph the Committee shall cooperate with the State Party concerned.

4. After examining the findings of its inquiry, made in accordance with paragraphs 2 and 3 of this article, the Committee shall transmit these findings to the State Party concerned together with any comments or recommendations which seem appropriate in view of the situation.

5. All the proceedings of the Committee referred to in paragraphs 1 to 4 of this article shall be confidential. After such proceedings have been completed with regard to an inquiry made in accordance with paragraph 3, the Committee may decide to include a summary account of the results of the proceedings in its annual report.]

[Article 6]

[The provisions of the present Protocol shall apply to the States Parties in addition to the provisions of the Convention on the Rights of the Child.]

Article 7

1. The present Protocol is open for signature by any State which is a party to the Convention or has signed it.

2. The present Protocol is subject to ratification or open to accession by any State which has ratified or acceded to the Convention. Instruments of ratification or accession shall be deposited with the Secretary-General of the United Nations.
3. The Secretary-General of the United Nations in his capacity as the depositary of the Convention and the Protocol shall inform all States Parties to the Convention and all States which have signed the Convention of each instrument of ratification or accession to the Protocol.

Article 8

1. The present Protocol shall enter into force three months after the deposit of the tenth instrument of ratification or accession.
2. For each State ratifying the present Protocol or acceding to it after its entry into force, the present Protocol shall enter into force one month after the date of the deposit of its own instrument of ratification or accession.

Article 9

1. Any State Party may denounce the present Protocol at any time by written notification to the Secretary-General of the United Nations, who shall thereafter inform the other States Parties to the Convention and all States which have signed the Convention. Denunciation shall take effect one year after the date of receipt of the notification by the Secretary-General of the United Nations. If, however on the expiry of that year the denouncing State Party is engaged in armed conflict, the denunciation shall not take effect
before the end of the armed conflict.
2. Such a denunciation shall not have the effect of releasing the State Party from its obligations under this Protocol in regard to any act which occurs prior to the date at which the denunciation becomes effective. Nor shall such a denunciation prejudice in any way the continued consideration of any matter which is already under consideration by the Committee prior to the date at which the denunciation becomes effective.

Article 10

1. The present Protocol, of which the Arabic, Chinese, English, French, Russian and Spanish texts are equally authentic, shall be deposited in the archives of the United Nations together with the Convention on the Rights of the Child.
2. The Secretary-General of the United Nations shall transmit certified copies of this Protocol to all States Parties to the Convention and all States which have signed the Convention.